Y0-CCH-645

ASPECTUS
ET
AFFECTUS

Essays and Editions
in Grosseteste and Medieval Intellectual Life
in Honor of

Richard C. Dales

edited by
Gunar Freibergs

with an Introduction by
Sir Richard W. Southern

AMS PRESS
NEW YORK

B
765
.G74
A86
1993

Library of Congress Cataloging-in-Publication Data

Aspectus et affectus : essays and editions in Grosseteste and Medieval intellectual life in honor of Richard C. Dales / edited by Gunar Freibergs : with an introduction by Richard W. Southern.
(AMS studies in the Middle Ages : no. 23)
Includes bibliographical references and index.
ISBN 0-404-64163-6
1. Grosseteste, Robert, 1175?–1253. 2. Europe—Intellectual life. 3. Philosophy, Medieval. I. Dales, Richard C. II. Freibergs, Gunar. III. Series.
B765.G74A86 1993
189'.4—dc20 91-57962
CIP

All AMS books are printed on acid-free paper that meets the guidelines for performance and durability of the Committee on Production Guidelines for Book Longevity of the Council on Library Resources.

COPYRIGHT © 1993 BY AMS PRESS, INC.
All rights reserved

AMS PRESS
56 East 13th Street
New York, N.Y. 10003, U.S.A.

Manufactured in the United States of America

Contents

Preface

This spring Richard C. Dales will have completed the sixty-fifth year of a life dedicated to stripping away the veil of obscurity from the intellectual history of the Middle Ages. It is an occasion which his colleagues and students recognized as an opportunity for a special celebration. Since the mark of a great teacher is the ability to inspire interest and excellence in others, then the greatest tribute they in turn can pay him is to produce evidence of that gift. This collection of essays and editions, which in subject, scope and content reflects the kind of scholarly endeavors in which Dales himself has been engaged for close to four decades, it is hoped, will constitute such evidence.

Many thanks are due to all the contributors, as well as to those colleagues who could not participate, but supported this project in spirit. Special thanks go to James K. Otte and Glenn M. Edwards for helping to get the project started and for their editorial suggestions. A particular vote of gratitude is due Elwood E. Mather, his wife Sharon, and Norice Bauer of Universal Intergraphix Corporation for transforming the manuscripts into laserprint works of art. Much credit is also owed to Paul W. Knoll for placing the resources of the Department of History at the University of Southern California behind the endeavor, and for shepherding it from start to finish. This project also benefited materially from a generous subvention provided by the Division of Social Sciences and Communication in the College of Letters, Arts and Sciences of the University of Southern California; many thanks to the dean of this division, C. Sylvester Whitaker, for his support. The biggest thanks must go, however, to the recipient himself, without whose fundamental inspiration and guidance a considerable amount of the knowledge and skill necessary for this project could not have materialized.

Gunar Freibergs
Los Angeles, 1991

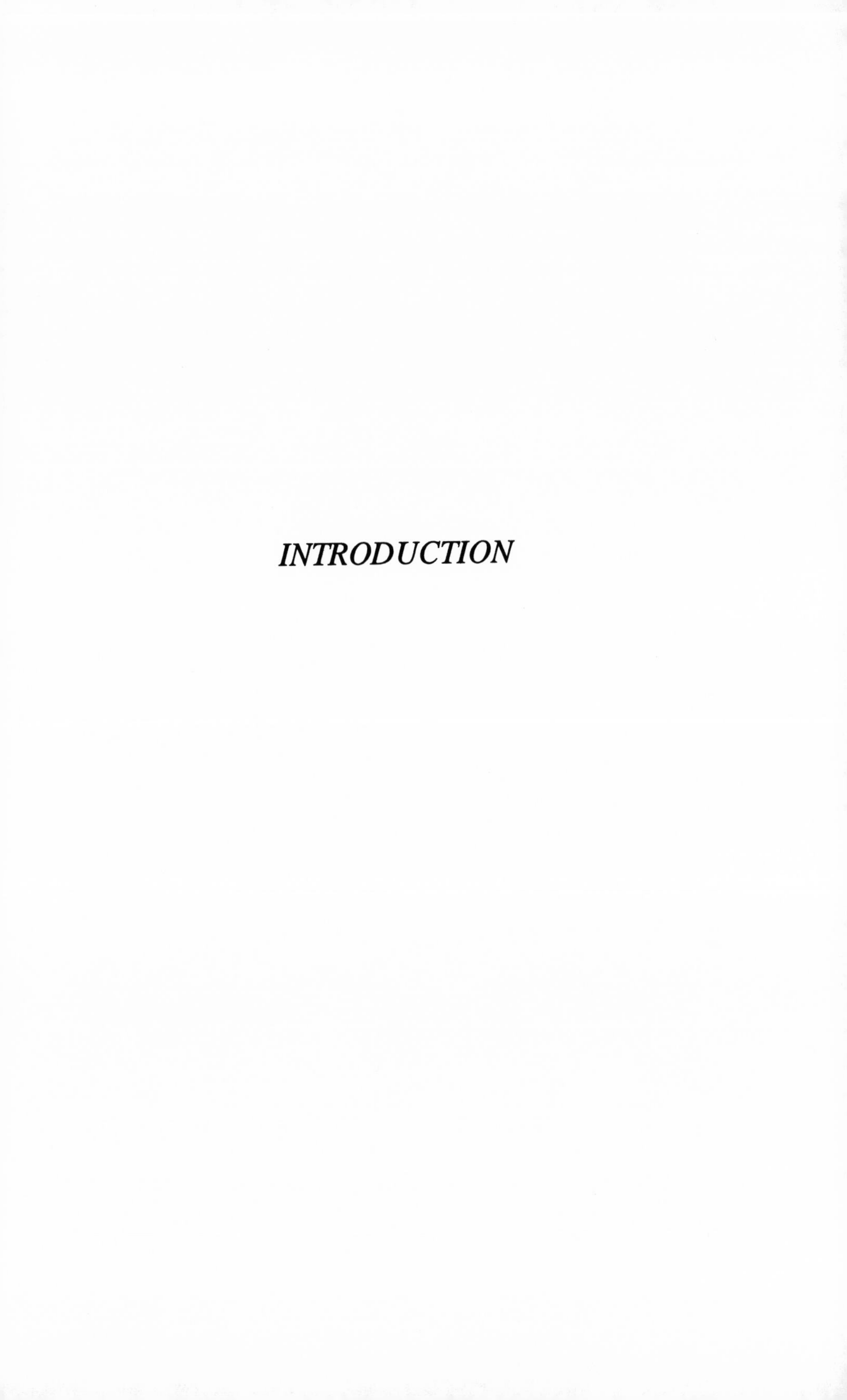

INTRODUCTION

Richard Dales and the Editing of Robert Grosseteste

Sir Richard W. Southern

Why Richard Dales, who was born in Akron, Ohio and took his baccalaureate at the University of Rochester, decided to go to Colorado for his Master of Arts degree, I do not know. Suffice it to say that it was an inspired decision, and this volume which has been written to honor his contribution to medieval scholarship, and especially to the study of the life and works of Robert Grosseteste, is one of its consequences. For it was at the University of Colorado that he found and understood the importance of one of the most remarkable scholarly initiatives in medieval studies in this century. I refer, of course, to S. Harrison Thomson; and not chiefly to his large and expansive personality, but to the vision and energy which led him to make a collection of materials, and especially of photographs of manuscripts, from nearly all the main libraries of Europe.[1]

The Colorado Hoard

Thomson's collection was made with a clearly conceived purpose of serving as the basis for surveying and editing the widely distributed and astonishingly numerous works of two deeply disturbing medieval personalities: Robert Grosseteste and John Wyclyf. In the 1930s, when the collection was chiefly made, it required great strength of conviction and determination to undertake such an operation. The literary output of both authors had been very large, and so the manuscript material which Harrison Thomson sought was widely scattered in libraries from Portugal to Poland, much of it in small collections which were difficult to track down and not easily available even when reached. The necessary photographic equipment was still rather primitive, as anyone who looks at the now decaying products of that time will realize. And, more daunting still, the whole idea of systematic photography of large quantities of manuscripts cut across the grain of the learned habits of those days. It was really rather provokingly "American." The likelihood of war and the probability of widespread destruction were in everybody's mind, but medieval manuscripts were not high on the list of many people's worries. Harrison Thomson, however, persisted and was justified by the event.

Although all the manuscript collections of Europe were soon put out of commission for six or seven years and there were some deeply deplorable losses, most of their contents survived. Nevertheless, though the worst had not happened, Harrison Thomson's vision meant that a large part of the original material for the study of the works of Grosseteste and Wyclyf was already stored at Colorado by the time that the Second World War broke out. In the years immediately after the War, when access to European manuscripts was still uncertain, Richard Dales was one of the first to understand the meaning of the whole operation, and to make it his life's work, first to use, then to understand, and above all to seek to convey to others, the meaning of the great mass of material that lay before him.

The authors whose works were collected in what I call the Colorado hoard would not at first sight seem an obvious choice for such a peaceful scholar. Grosseteste and Wyclyf were both turbulent characters. But behind their troubled personalities, buried in the mass of materials which they left behind, there lay a unique opportunity for studying several aspects of the central medieval tradition of religious and scientific thought.

I do not know whether the young Dales ever contemplated making Wyclyf, instead of Grosseteste, the subject of his life's work, but I am sure that he made the right choice. His main interest has always lain in the central tradition of the medieval West, and within Grosseteste's personality there was a deeper centrality than is to be found in Wyclyf. Also, Grosseteste had a scientific curiosity and love of the physical universe, which Wyclyf lacked. These two sides -- his centrality and his scientific insight -- are reflected in all Richard's work, and at every step he has related Grosseteste to the central tradition of European scientific and religious thought.

The editing of any medieval text, indeed, requires unremitting attention to details in the text and in the interpretation of the author's words. But, in Grosseteste's case, the difficulties are multiplied by his habits as an author. There is no question that one of his most impressive characteristics is an instinct for great issues. But he somewhat resembles Aristotle in possessing an intellectual force which cannot be confined within a literary form. It would not be true to say that he adorned whatever he touched, for his works are often far from elegant. In particular, his habit of continuing to correct and add to what he had written, and often leaving it in the end incomplete, makes it immensely difficult to present the developing text in a neat printed form. He left nearly all subjects more untidy than he found them. Then too, his works present other difficulties to an unusual extent: most of them are preserved in manuscripts far removed in time and place from his own life; attributions are often uncertain or absent, and the copies abound in errors. I do not think that any other major medieval figure left his work in such disarray or subject to so many hazards of destruction or deformation, and it is the first task of an editor to bring order out of an untidy mass of loose ends. The transfer of material, and especially material in process of development, from the written to the printed page raises questions of great delicacy, which are often incapable of a fully satisfactory answer. Not many of those who see only the finished result can appreciate the difficulties which Grosseteste bequeathed to his editors. Grosseteste himself narrowly failed to achieve canonization, for a reason which Fr. Daniel Callus explained with sweet and conclusive simplicity: "He was not a saint." But his editors need to be saints, and I shall be a ready witness in the process of Richard's editorial beatification. For his first study, he chose a work which demanded a wide view of the medieval intellectual tradition: Grosseteste's *Commentary on Aristotle's Physics*. It is a work which represented the accumulated, and never finally finished, efforts of many years of Grosseteste's life. It also presented formidable textual problems, being ill-preserved in three horribly defective manuscripts, of which the best combined Grosseteste's *Commentary on the Physics* with his treatise on the eternity of the world. The responsibility of editing such a work might have daunted anyone, but Richard brought to the task a method which he has steadily pursued and refined from 1952 to the present day. On the one hand, he has concentrated on making hitherto unknown or little known, unprinted or badly printed, texts available for scholarly examination in editions based on all the known manuscripts, which will serve the needs of scholars for a very long time. On the other, he has discussed with unremitting care and fairness of judgement the general background of the problems on which Grosseteste left remarks, which are always penetrating, often original, sometimes extraordinarily far-sighted, but all too often incomplete and still in process of development. Richard's patience, open-mindedness, understanding of the main issues, and readiness to return again and again to unsolved problems are all deeply imprinted on my memory. The works in which I have seen his editorial labors at closest quarters are the *Hexaëmeron* (deservedly the best seller in the series in which it appeared), *De cessatione legalium*, and *De decem mandatis*. They form only one part of his editorial labors, but, concealed within the clarity of the printed page, and in some of the inevitable mistakes which can so easily be spotted on the printed page, there is a tale of countless problems which required and elicited editorial qualities of a very high order.

The works I have just mentioned have one thing in common: they represent a distinct epoch in Grosseteste's life. They were written in his "Oxford" years (from about 1225 to 1235), a time filled with a uniquely original and diversified range of intellectual activities, too varied to bring all, or even any, of them to a state of final resolution. This is when he was chiefly occupied with biblical and theological questions, when he pushed a little further his burgeoning vision of the primary role of light in the created universe, when he began the study of Greek and his translation of the *Hierarchies* of pseudo-Dionysius, and when he also made the latest additions to his unfinished *Commentary on Aristotle's Physics*. This was the quintessential Grosseteste:

always more interested in thinking and writing about great issues than in presenting posterity with finished works.

It was in editing the *Commentary on the Physics* that Richard also began to write about some of the great issues which occupied Grosseteste in his later years. A central place in the labors of his editor, as of Grosseteste himself, has been occupied by the relations between time and eternity. Grosseteste's penetrating interest in this problem provides a good illustration of two of his leading characteristics -- his natural gravitation towards the most profound and difficult aspects of every subject that he studied, and his power of combining a concrete grasp of detail with a visionary sense of the ever-present spiritual universe. Richard Dales has made outstanding contributions to both areas, and I can do no more here by way of illustration than examine a few of the steps in Grosseteste's career which led him to become engaged in these problems.

Time and Eternity

The doctrine that the physical universe had no beginning is a conspicuous feature of Aristotle's *Physics*, on which Grosseteste provided the first medieval Latin commentary. Nevertheless, although the *Physics* had not been available to western scholars in the twelfth century, it was known that it contained a doctrine of the eternity of the universe which appeared to contradict both the account of the creation in the Bible and in Plato's *Timaeus*, which had emerged in the early twelfth century as the fundamental source of western cosmology. Despite this apparent conflict, enlightened scholars of the early twelfth century, such as Thierry of Chartres and William of Conches, had found a way of harmonizing the accounts of the creation in Plato, Aristotle and the Bible. They had done this by arguing that Aristotle's account of the eternity of the universe did not mean that the universe had no beginning, but only that its beginning was coincident with the beginning of time. With this gloss, Aristotle's claim meant only that there was no time before the creation. Thus it was possible to avoid the unacceptable conclusion that the world and God were coeternal.[2]

This harmonizing of Plato, Aristotle and Christianity played an important part in the twelfth-century effort to reconcile secular learning with Christian doctrine, which is rightly considered one of the most attractive features of the century, and Richard Dales's investigations, soon to be crowned by a general study of the whole subject, have made a lasting contribution to this area of medieval intellectual history. But the texts of Grosseteste which he has edited have demonstrated that Grosseteste had no patience either with the attempt at reconciliation or with the manner in which it was realized by his predecessors. It will suffice here to quote a single sentence of his *Hexaëmeron*: "Let those who strive to make Aristotle a Christian beware that they do not make themselves heretics."[3]

I have nothing to add to Richard Dales's account of the general scene, but there may still be something to be learnt about the light that Grosseteste's rejection of the consensus of the previous century throws on his personal development. In particular, we may ask: under what influences did he so energetically denounce the unifying impulse which had been dear to the hearts of the humanists of the previous century?

Of course it is clear that his impatience with the advocates of reconciliation came partly from his knowing much more about Aristotle's thought than the scholars of the previous century. Quite apart from his knowing (as they did not) the Latin text of Aristotle's *Physics*, he was also able to speak with some disdain of his predecessors' ignorance of Greek, of which he himself did not yet know much. But what was much more important in provoking his hostile reaction to the consensus of the previous century was the course of theological reading that he had undertaken during the ten years before writing his *Hexaëmeron*. During these years he had studied with all his immense powers of application a large part of the theological writings of both the Latin and Greek Fathers. He knew what they had thought about Aristotle's view of the eternity of the world. And, most important of all for our present purpose, he had already begun to study the works of pseudo-Dionysius in Greek and had probably taken his first steps in making a new translation of the pseudo-Dionysian corpus.

These new sources had immensely enlarged the dimensions of his thoughts: he inhabited an intellectual world more varied than any of his immediate predecessors, and his growing mastery of Greek gave him a new sense of the past. In addition, there was his new breadth of subject matter. Broadly speaking, from having (before about 1220) been almost wholly concerned with the task of understanding the phenomena of the physical universe, his recent course of theological reading had enlarged his intellectual horizon to embrace also the whole range of problems concerned with creation and redemption, and to give him a new vision of divine illumination flowing down to fill the created universe, and the minds of those who raised their eyes to God, with light.

As a small but significant consequence of this enlargement, he now began to give a new application to a maxim which he had frequently used in the past with (as we shall see) a more limited understanding of its meaning. The maxim may be expressed thus: "The mind's range of vision cannot extend further than its range of love." He had often in the past, when his mind was wholly engaged in secular subjects, applied this maxim to the task of enlarging his understanding of the physical world. But he was now able to see that it had much wider implications. Philosophers, he now declared, were bound to fall into error on the question of creation, because -- being accustomed to look no further than the world of transitory things -- they were incapable of loving, and therefore of thinking properly about, the nature of God and of the universe beyond space and time.[4]

Moreover, he now saw that this failure was also associated with Aristotle's fundamental error about the eternity of the created universe: it arose from his misapplication of a logical doctrine, which may be expressed thus: "An effect is necessarily coexistent with its cause unless there is either a defect of power in the cause or a defect of potentiality in the material on which the cause operates."[5] If this doctrine is applied to the creation of the universe, it must follow that the universe is coexistent with God throughout eternity, for there could be no delay arising from defect in the cause (which is God), nor could it arise from any defect in the material from which the universe was created, for it was created from nothing. It was clear, therefore, that Aristotle -- despite the explanation of his twelfth-century defenders -- thought that the universe was coexistent with God; and it was also clear why he was bound to think this.[6]

At a single stroke, therefore, Grosseteste destroyed one of the finest flowers of reconciliatory twelfth-century humanism. Nevertheless, his argument left him with two problems. The first was: how could Aristotle and his Christian defenders have made such a mistake? In answer to this, Grosseteste could invoke the principle that the mind can see no further than it can love. Therefore philosophers, whether Christian or pagan, can see no further than they can love; and if their thoughts are fixed only on earthly things, they will understand nothing beyond. Consequently they will suppose that the logic of time and space applies equally in eternity.

So much for the first problem. But the second is more serious. Aristotle's logical principle that every effect must be coexistent with its cause unless there is an impediment either in the power of the cause or in the suitability of the material seems essentially incontrovertible. Are we therefore compelled to accept that, in speaking of God and the creation, we have reached a point at which the rules of logic no longer apply?

Grosseteste met this difficulty by announcing another principle to which he had perhaps been guided by studying and translating the works of pseudo-Dionysius. He declared that Aristotle's logical law of cause and effect is applicable only in situations in which cause and effect are "of the same measure."[7]

These two lines of objection to Aristotle's argument -- namely the failure of his mental *affectus* to provide the necessary enlargement for his mental *aspectus*, and his failure to recognize the different "measures" to which the cause and effect of the creation of the universe belong -- raise some interesting problems about the chronology, sources and subject-matter of Grosseteste's intellectual development. I believe that these problems will only be finally solved when we have modern editions of all Grosseteste's works. But some provisional remarks can be made which may help to show how much has already been achieved by recent editors, and in particular by

Richard Dales, and how much still remains to be done. I shall begin first with the *aspectus-affectus* nexus.

I do not know of any passage in which Grosseteste elaborated the nature of the "measures" which had to be "equal" for the rule of cause and effect to apply, but it is fairly clear that he meant that the cause and its effect must be on the same ontological level for Aristotle's law to be applicable. That is to say, the cause and its effect must both belong either to the world of space and time, or to the universe of pure essences, or to that still more ethereal state of the divine being. But a cause which has its effect in a different order of being is not bound by Aristotle's principle of the simultaneity of cause and effect. The flaw, therefore, both in Aristotle and in his Christian adherents, lay in their inability to discern the different levels, or "measures," of existence about which they were presuming to speak. And this was another example of the principle that "the range of the mind's sight can extend no further than the range of its love." It followed from this that both Aristotle and his Christian defenders of the previous century had failed to extend their *affectus mentis* beyond the range of time and space to the "measure" of the eternal world.

In his *Hexaëmeron*, Grosseteste used both these lines of argument -- the limitation of the mind's *aspectus* by the range of its *affectus*, and the limitation of the rule of cause and effect to things of equal measure; and the interesting point about the appearance of both of them at this stage in his life and not before is that they show him standing at a cross-road in his intellectual career. As we shall see, the *aspectus-affectus* association goes back to early interests in the liberal arts. But, his doctrine of the "different measures" of eternal being and created things reflects his theological and Greek studies during the eight or ten years before he wrote his *Hexaëmeron*. As its immediate source, I am inclined to think that he learnt it from pseudo-Dionysius, whose introductory treatise, *De divinis nominibus*, is filled with discussion on the different measures of participation in the divine nature granted by God to the different hierarchies of created beings.[8] By the time that he wrote his *Hexaëmeron*, Grosseteste had already begun his study, and perhaps even his translation, of the pseudo-Dionysian *Hierarchies*.[9]

In the present state of the texts, this suggestion must remain very tentative. But if it proves to be correct, one of Grosseteste's two explanations of Aristotle's error, namely his confusion of two different and incompatible "measures" of existence, is new and comes from Grosseteste's recent study of pseudo-Dionysius; and the other -- the failure of the philosophers' affective love to extend their mental range beyond the sphere of worldly affairs -- goes back to an early period in Grosseteste's intellectual development, when he was chiefly concerned with astrology, astronomy and the liberal arts, and it forms a link between the two main phases of his intellectual career.[10]

A Turning Point in Grosseteste's Intellectual Odyssey

If we trace the evolution of *aspectus* and *affectus mentis* in Grosseteste's thought backwards from his *Hexaëmeron* and *Commentary on Aristotle's Physics*, we come to his *Commentary on the Posterior Analytics* of about 1220. In this work, he took great pains to explain that the mind cannot argue about general concepts when its *aspectus*, or range of vision, is still clouded by the confused assault of corporeal images.[11] It is only when this limitation has been overcome by purifying the mind from sensual lusts, and by engaging in calm consideration, that the mind's *affectus* can rise from the chaos of sense impressions to the clarity of the general laws of which these sense impressions are the harbingers. Following this clue, Grosseteste had been able to give a brilliantly clear account of the way in which the confusion of sense impressions could be gradually clarified until the mind became familiar with the laws of nature of which sense impressions were the indicators.

In Grosseteste's account of the way in which sense impressions provided the data for general laws, there was as yet no question of the mind passing beyond the "measure" of space and time: sense impressions and the laws which they reflected all belonged to the same "measure." All that the mind needed for grasping the general laws behind the sense impressions was sharper vision, greater discipline, and freedom from confusion and turbulent desires, to arrive at that sudden wonderful insight into the regularities of nature which has been the reward of scientific patience at all times.

As he studied and commented on Aristotle's *Posterior Analytics*, Grosseteste reached his maturity as a scientist, and at that time he looked no further. The cure for the confusions which were the first result of the flood of sense impressions assaulting the mind had not to be sought outside the system of temporal-spatial impressions. So he had nothing to say about events at different ontological levels; but, within the limits of time and space, the broadening *affectus* of the disciplined mind leads the observer on from the most elementary impressions to a general view extending to the limits of time and space. It is important that the whole movement starts with the assault of sense impressions which awaken the mind from sleep and set it on its voyage of discovery, comparing one impression with another, distinguishing color from magnitude and magnitude from substance, and thus arriving at general laws which cover the whole field of time and space. This acknowledged primacy of sense impressions was Grosseteste's greatest breakaway from the conventional distrust of the senses, and the greatest contribution which the *Posterior Analytics* made to his development was in revealing to him that the confusion of sense impressions brings its own cure by leading the mind to make distinctions and thus allow the broadening *affectus* of the mind to arrive at a knowledge of general laws. In a splendid passage, he declared his scientific faith: "Reason sleeps until it is awakened by the senses."[12] It is by the continual battering of sense impressions that the mind begins to have the possibility of seeing into the true nature of things; and, as the mind begins to find the explanation of the multiple sense impressions, it begins to love that which is greater than itself.

Here then, in about 1220, we already have the double role of the mind's *aspectus* and *affectus* clearly distinguished as mutually supporting faculties of the mind. But these faculties are still operating within the single field of time and space. When the mind stretches further out beyond time and space, and attempts to make statements about the relations between God and the created universe, the logical structure which suffices for a description of this world becomes inadequate. This does not mean that nothing can be said about the relations between God and the created universe. Some of Grosseteste's most original thoughts about the role of light in coming out from God to fill the whole universe, and the role of the incarnation in completing the human nature, which had been created to know God, were devoted to the study of the ways in which light and incarnation formed a bridge between eternity and the created universe of time and space.

This new movement, however, comes from above, and not from below like the movement which leads to scientific truths. These later developments would carry us into a new field of inquiry, and I turn back to the two decades before 1220 and ask whether there are any earlier appearances of *aspectus* and *affectus* in Grosseteste's account of the way in which human knowledge grows.

During these years there are no works of similar magnitude to the *Commentary on the Posterior Analytics*, but there are several small tracts which provide some clues to his mental development and to the gradual change in the range of his observations and the generalizations which he based upon them.

The most important of these small works for our purpose is his *De artibus liberalibus*, in which he sketched the use of the liberal arts in developing mankind's capacity to live in sympathetic harmony with the natural world. This process, like that later to be described in the growth of scientific understanding, is also brought about by the interaction of the mind's *aspectus* and *affectus*. But here the mind's *aspectus* is not concerned with sense impressions, but with the doctrines of the individual liberal arts; and the mind's *affectus* is the more generalized activity of applying the doctrine of a particular art to the needs of life. At one point, Grosseteste ascribes to rhetoric the function of acting as intermediary between the *aspectus*, or knowledge, of grammar and its application to the needs of life. And the function which rhetoric performs in adapting grammar to the needs of life, music and astronomy similarly apply to the doctrines of medicine. So already here, though much less coherently than in his *Commentary on the Posterior*

Analytics or in the still later *Hexaëmeron*, he envisioned the *aspectus* of mind as the elementary stage of knowledge, and its *affectus* as the mature consideration which makes knowledge useful for living.[13]

One conclusion which emerges from an examination of the *De artibus liberalibus* is that, although Grosseteste already envisages a movement from *aspectus* to *affectus*, in making detailed truths available for human life, his thinking on the subject is much less clear than in his *Commentary on the Posterior Analytics*. And, some ten years later still, when he wrote his *Hexaëmeron*, his field of knowledge has transformed its extension beyond the limits of time and space, when the growth of knowledge by illumination from above was, in some degree at least, replacing the ascent from sense impressions to general principles which had been the main movement in his earlier thought.

The Achievement of Grosseteste's Editors

If I labor these small points, I do so mainly to display one small part of the benefits which the study of Grosseteste's intellectual development has received and will in increasing measure receive in future, from new editions of his works. The editors of his extraordinarily scattered literary remains are taking the first and most difficult steps along the long road which will lead in the course of time to our understanding one of the longest, most varied, and most powerful intellectual developments of any single individual in medieval history. We owe it chiefly to editors during the past fifty years that we can begin to draw the outline of Grosseteste's long effort of intellectual exploration, but it may require another fifty years of editorial labors before it becomes possible to give a full and detailed account of his many-sided voyage of discovery.

I do not suggest that, when this time comes, Grosseteste will turn out to have been a philosopher or imaginative writer of the stature of Thomas Aquinas or Dante. But I am sure that he will be increasingly revealed as a uniquely powerful and independent interpreter of the learning and experience of the first half of the thirteenth century. No other individual embraced so powerfully, or with such independent power, the whole range of contemporary learning, passing successively from music and medicine, to astronomy and astrology, to the study of the scientific method of Aristotle, to the Latin and Greek Fathers, and beyond them to translating and commenting on the *Hierarchies* of pseudo-Dionysius and Aristotle's *Ethics*. The range of Grosseteste's independent effort is astonishing; and, what is even more astonishing, much of his intellectual work was done while he was immersed, to an extent unequalled among even the most dedicated bishops of his time, in the severe, rigorous, and imaginative administration of the biggest diocese in England, bringing to his work also an energy and personal vision which brought him into headlong conflict equally with royal and papal administration and with the general direction of papal government.

There are still many gaps for future editors to fill, but some features of the general outline are becoming plain. We can begin to see that Grosseteste's uniquely varied and long-continued journey of discovery contains many strange twists of fortune, and that, chaotic though the material is that allows us to follow in his footsteps, it will one day tell a story of a mind of very great vigor and independence, covering a wider range of subjects over a longer period than any other medieval character who has left a record of his activity.

When all his works have been critically edited, as one day they will be, Grosseteste will come into full view, with a degree of detail not yet available, and with a range of intellectual vision not yet fully explored, as one of the giants of medieval Europe, and Richard Dales will have an eminent place among those who have made this possible.

Notes

[1] For the contents of the collection, see the *Inventory of the S. Harrison Thomson Collection of Photostats and Microfilms of Grosseteste, Wyclyf, and other English Medieval MSS*, compiled by Scott Dickerson, for the Joseph Regenstein Library, University of Chicago Library, Department of Special Collections, Chicago, 1982.

[2] For Richard Dales's contribution to the study of this whole subject, see the Bibliography at the end of this volume, especially articles 21, 30, 32, and the recent volume, *Medieval Discussions on the Eternity of the World*, Leiden, 1989.

[3] Robert Grosseteste, *Hexaëmeron* 1.8.4, ed. Richard C. Dales and Servus Gieben, Auctores Britannici Medii Aevi 6 (London, 1982), p. 61.

[4] See Robert Grosseteste, *Commentarius in VIII libros physicorum Aristotelis* 8, ed. Richard C. Dales (Boulder, 1963), p. 147: "Necesse fuit philosophos in hunc errorem (concerning the perpetuity of the world) incidere, quia ab errore de perpetuitate et infinitate motus et temporis ex parte ante et ex parte post nullus potest scientifice liberari nisi qui potest simplicitatem eternitatis intelligere; sed cum mentis aspectus, vel intelligentia, non possit superius ascendere quam ascendat eius affectus vel appetitus. Philosophorum autem affectus ligati erant plus cum transitoriis quam cum eternis, immo illorum apprehensio in phantasmatibus mutabilium detenta, simplicitatem eternitatis attingere non potuit. Necesse igitur fuit eis ut ante omne tempus ymaginarentur tempus aliud, et sic ante omnem motum ymaginarentur motum alium, sicut homines extra celum ymaginantur spacium et extra illud spacium aliud spacium, et sic in infinitum. Et hec falsa ymaginacio infinitatis temporis ex parte ante inducit necessario falsam ymaginacionem perpetuitatis motus et mundi et creature coequeve deo." In his *Hexaëmeron*, p. 61, Grosseteste gives a similar account of *affectus* and *aspectus*; but see nn. 11 and 13 for somewhat different accounts at earlier stages in his career.

[5] *Commentarius in VIII libros physicorum Aristotelis* 8 (p. 148): "Hec autem propositio, 'omne quod de potentia priori exit in actum,' sic probatur; cum aliquid est in potencia et nondum egreditur ad actum, aut hoc est quia causa efficiens nondum est, aut si est, quia insufficiens est aut impeditur, aut quia illud in quod agat efficiens nondum est, aut si hoc fuerit, quia agens et illud in quod agat disiuncta sunt."

[6] *Hexaëmeron* 1.8.5 (p. 61): "Decepti erant (philosophi) quoque argumento illo quo dicebant: 'tota et plena causa cui nullam oportet adicere condicionem ad hoc ut agat existente, necessarium esse totum et plenum effectum eiusdem cause simul semper cum ea coexistere.' Deus autem talis causa est . . . Quapropter, si mundus ab eo factus est, semper cum eo coexistit."

[7] Ibid. 1.8.5-6 (pp. 61-62): "Decepti erant (philosophi) quoque argumento illo quo dicebant: 'tota et plena causa cui nullam oportet adicere condicionem ad hoc ut agat existente, necessarium esse totum et plenum effectum eiusdem cause simul semper cum ea coexistere.'. . . (Sed non) intelligunt quod verbum 'coexistencie simul pleni effectus cum plena causa' implicat causam et effectum sub eiusdem generis cadere mensuram, utpote quod ambo sint temporalia vel ambo eterna."

[8] For Grosseteste's translation, see *De divinis nominibus*, in *Dionysiana: le texte latin des oeuvres du ps. Ar<a>eopagite*, vol. 1, ed. P. Chevallier, Paris, 1927. For the importance of *mensura* in this part of pseudo-Dionysius, see R. Rogues, *L'univers dionysien* (Lille, 1954), pp. 59-67.

[9] See. *Hexaëmeron*, pp. xxii, 78-79, 262.

[10] Since my remarks in what follows are somewhat at variance with the account in James McEvoy, *The Philosophy of Robert Grosseteste* (Oxford, 1983), I may briefly mention my reasons for suggesting a different approach, as follows: McEvoy, p. 258, suggests that Grosseteste's use of *affectus* and *aspectus* is based on Augustine, *Soliloquia* 1.6 (PL 32:875-76). But Augustine in this passage speaks only of *affectus mentis* which he equates with reason, and says nothing about the association with *aspectus mentis* which is central to Grosseteste's earlier view of intellectual progress. McEvoy (pp. 107, 135, 138) quotes several passages in Grosseteste's commentary on pseudo-Dionysius' *Celestial Hierarchy* to substantiate his view of the *aspectus-affectus* linkage in this work, but Grosseteste does not make this conjunction in any of them. All the passages quoted by McEvoy are concerned with the outpouring of light as the first constituent of the universe. Very tentatively, I am inclined to think that Grosseteste's growing preoccupation with the outpouring of light as the essential link between God and the creation largely replaced his earlier conception of the mind extending its range by the upward *aspectus-affectus* movement. But for greater clarity on this point Professor McEvoy's edition of Grosseteste's *Commentary on Galatians* must be awaited.

[11] *Commentarius in posteriorum analyticorum libros* 1.14, ed. Pietro Rossi (Florence, 1981), p. 215-16: "Ratio enim in nobis sopita non agit nisi postquam per sensus operationem, cui admiscetur, fuerit expergefacta. Causa autem quare obnubilatur visus anime per molem corporis corrupti est quod affectus et aspectus anime non sunt divisi, nec attingit aspectus eius nisi quo attingit affectus sive amor eius. Cum igitur amor et affectus anime convertitur ad corpus et ad illecebras corporales necessario trahit secum aspectum et avertit eum a suo lumine, quod se habet ad ipsum sicut sol se habet ad oculos exteriores.

[12] Ibid. 1.14 (p. 215).

[13] *De artibus liberalibus*: "Aspectus vero primo aspicit; secundo aspectu seu cognita verificat, et cum verificata fuerint apud mentem seu aspectum convenientia seu nociva, inhiat affectus ad amplexandum convenientia, vel in seipsum retrahit ut fugiat nociva," *Die Philosophischen Werke des Robert Grosseteste, Bischofs von Lincoln*, ed. Ludwig Baur, Beiträge zur Geschichte der Philosophie des Mittelalters 9, (Münster i. W., 1912), p. 1.

Part 1

ROBERT GROSSETESTE

Robert Grosseteste and Adam Marsh on Light in a Summary Attributed to St. Bonaventure

Servus Gieben, O.F.M. Cap.

By his repeated conjunction of the name of Adam Marsh with that of Robert Grosseteste, Roger Bacon has caused a good deal of worry to the students of the early Franciscan School at Oxford. This observation should not be misunderstood. Grosseteste and the friar were lifelong friends. They freely associated with each other and shared their intimate intellectual and moral problems in their correspondence.[1] Their intense cooperation in pastoral and political affairs cannot be brought up for discussion. The embarrassing question is another. Roger Bacon explicitly and repeatedly puts Adam Marsh on a par with Grosseteste in such issues as the knowledge of foreign languages[2] and the acquaintance with natural and mathematical sciences.[3] Someone may speculate that those characteristics were probably distinguishing works of Adam Marsh which are now lost. But, in point of fact, it remains disappointing to find that in his large collection of letters, which does survive, there is nothing to suggest his knowledge of natural science and languages to which Roger Bacon bears such enthusiastic testimony.[4]

About twenty-five years ago, when studying a pseudo-Bonaventurian work called *Symbolica theologia,* the writer was unexpectedly struck again with the conjunction of the names of Robert Grosseteste and Adam Marsh, but this time in a quite different context.[5] In the course of a long discussion on the proper and metaphorical names of the angels, spelled out in no less than nineteen chapters, the anonymous author arrived at chapter nine, which he entitled: "How the natural properties of light are appropriate to angels."[6] Here he intended to explain in what ways the natural properties of corporeal light could be transferred to the angels which are spiritual light. In doing so, he declared: "I shall take care to designate some of their properties according as I found them introduced in the writings of famous doctors, namely of the bishop of Lincoln and of friar Adam Marsh."[7] The summary that follows is a thorough schematic outline of the doctrine of light. At first sight, the texts offered in this part seem to be almost completely borrowed from the *Hexaëmeron* of Robert Grosseteste, specifically from chapter ten of the second part.[8] Apparently, no other work of the bishop has been directly involved. On second thought, however, several particularities emerged, which it has been impossible to verify in any of Grosseteste's writings. Relying on what this informant tells about his sources, it must be assumed that these parts come from the pen of

Adam Marsh. Possibly the matter may even be taken a step further. In view of the fact that the anonymous author of *Symbolica theologia* does not qualify himself to the reader as a man of great synthetic thought, -- he rather presents himself as a collector of biblical texts suitable to his mystical interpretations[9] -- it is quite possible that the whole of the neat schematic outline on the doctrine of light was compiled from another author, perhaps from Adam Marsh himself, who had a genuine talent of making similar summaries.[10] In his abstract of Grosseteste's chapter on light, he had noticed that the bishop distinguished twenty different modes appropriate to spiritual things.[11] Did he organize them into a logical composition?

Outlining a Theory of Corporeal Light

The best way to show the synthetic qualities of the summary under consideration might be to offer a diagram of its structure. It proceeds as follows. After a short introduction on the goodness of light, with an intriguing quotation from St. Basil and another from St. Ambrose, the author, in the way seen before, refers to his sources, Robert Grosseteste and Adam Marsh. Next, he proposes the main division of his subject. Corporeal light, he proposes, can be viewed in a fourfold way, namely according to its substance (*secundum substantiam*), to its virtue (*secundum virtutem*), to its appearance (*secundum speciem*) and to its operations (*secundum operationem*). In conformity with this plan he develops his theme in this manner:[12]

1. Light, according to its substance, is:
   1.1 noble in its origin (*origine nobilis*)
   1.2 substantial in its quiddity (*quidditate substantialis*)
   1.3 subtle in its essence (*essentia subtilis*)

2. Light, according to its virtue, is:
   2.1 multipliable (*multiplicabilis*)
   2.2 inflexible (*inflexibilis*)
   2.3 incoercible (*incoarctabilis*)

3. Light, according to its appearance, is:
   3.1 in itself absolutely beautiful (*in se absolute pulchra*)
   3.2 in beautiful things causing beauty (*in pulchris effective pulchra*)
   3.3 in ugly things remaining beautiful (*in foedis mansive pulchra*)

4. Light, according to its operation, can be considered:
   4.1 absolutely in itself (*absolute in se*)
      4.1.1 at once it is and transmits (*simul est et gignit*)
      4.1.2 at once it transmits and diffuses itself (*simul gignit et se diffundit*)
      4.1.3 at once it diffuses itself and brightens (*simul se diffundit et clarescit*)
      4.1.4 it has these properties that:

4.1.4.1 it refuses itself to nothing (*nulli se negat*)
4.1.4.2 it manifests everything (*omnia manifestat*)
4.1.4.3 it distinguishes single things (*singula distinguit*)
4.2 relative to the being of things (*relate ad esse rerum*)
4.2.1 to things existing in the divine mind (*ad res existentes in mente divina*)
4.2.2 to the created dwelling of the blessed (*ad habitationem beatorum creatam*)
4.2.3 to the universe (*ad mundi machinam universam*)
4.2.3.1 to the minor world or man (*ad minorem mundum seu hominem*):
- as to the soul (*quantum ad animam*)
- as to the body (*quantum ad corpus*)
- as to the conjunction (*quantum ad coniunctum*)

4.2.3.2 to the major world or the whole mass of the world (*ad maiorem mundum seu totam molem mundi*):
- as to the region beyond heaven (*ad regionem supercaelestem*)
- as to the celestial region (*ad regionem caelestem*)
- as to the region beneath heaven (*ad regionem subcaelestem*)

To each point of the divisions a short explanation is added. This may be a text from the Bible, a quotation from the Fathers, or an argument borrowed from the writings of Grosseteste and Adam Marsh. It is difficult to see where the author, if at all, speaks on his own authority. Some of the author's explanations will now be discussed in more detail.

Sources and Authorities Quoted

The Bible texts, quoted in the summary, are partly well-known passages on light: Genesis 1.4, Ecclesiastes 11.7, John 8.12, Ephesians 5.13 and 1 John 1.5; or they deal with the heavenly city: Hebrews 11.10 and Apocalypse 21.23, and are thus closely related to light. Surprisingly, however, only three of these texts occur in the *Hexaëmeron* of Robert Grosseteste.[13] Did the anonymous author insert the other biblical passages on his own accord or did he find them cited in a work by Adam Marsh? For the moment the question must be left open.

From the very first quotation of a text from the Fathers the reader encounters a remarkable feature. Having taken as a starting point the goodness of the light (Gen. 1.4), in confirmation the author quotes a passage from St. Basil's *Hexaëmeron*. This work was heavily used by Grosseteste, but always in Eustathius' Latin paraphrase.[14] Only for Basil's homilies 10 and 11 Grosseteste made use of a Greek manuscript and presented translations of his own. In the present case, the quotation is from homily 2.7. The text offers two surprises: it is not included among the ninety-three citations in Grosseteste's *Hexaëmeron*, and it does not follow Eustathius' version. Since the quotation is not found in Grosseteste's commentary, the reader is again confronted with the question whether the anonymous author quotes St. Basil on his own account or on Adam Marsh's. This time the alternative should not be difficult. The quotation, instead of being in Eustathius' Latin paraphrase, exhibits the carefully accurate verbatim style which has always been associated with the Greek-Latin translations of Robert Grosseteste and his coadjutors. It is not probable and it may reasonably be excluded, that the man who compiled the *Symbolica theologia* was able and, if he was, would have found leisure to directly translate from the Greek manuscript a quotation which he might, or might not, insert in a specified chapter of his book. Most likely he borrowed the text from one of his informants, Grosseteste or Adam Marsh. The issue is important for both of them. For Grosseteste, since there is no indication that he made translations of any part of St. Basil's *Hexaëmeron*, except of some passages of the above mentioned homilies 10 and 11. For Adam Marsh, because there is no positive trace of his knowledge of languages, which was so highly extolled by Roger Bacon. But let the reader himself judge of the different qualities of the translation adopted in the *Symbolica theologia* and the old version of Eustathius.

Basil, *Hexaëmeron*:

> *῎Επειτα νῦν ἡ τοῦ θεοῦ κρίσις περὶ τοῦ καλοῦ, οὐ πάντως πρὸς τὸ ἐν ὄψει τερπνόν ἀποβλέποντος, ἀλλὰ καὶ πρὸς τὴν εἰς ὕστερον ἀπ' αὐτοῦ ὠφέλειαν προορωμένου γεγένηται.*[15]

Eustathius:

> Hujusmodi ergo Dei testimonium, non ad hoc solum respicit quod per se lux bona est et jucunda cernentibus, sed etiam propter utilitatem quae postmodum ex ea fuit collata mortalibus, bonam dixit.[16]

Symbolica theologia:

> Dei iudicium de bono non omnino ad illud quod in visu delectabile respicientis sed ad eam quae in posterum ab ipsa utilitatem praevidentis factum est.[17]

So far the reader has been left with the alternative of attributing the foregoing translation to Robert Grosseteste or to Adam Marsh. Yet, in the summary on light there is a second quotation from the *Hexaëmeron* of St. Basil. The passage is taken from the same context, just a few lines earlier in the seventh paragraph of the second homily. This time, however, also Grosseteste is reproducing the passage in his *Hexaëmeron*. Although his quotation presents some minor variants, he is clearly citing Eustathius' translation. The anonymous author, on the contrary, exhibits again the *ad litteram* version, so typical of Grosseteste's surrounding. These are the texts:

Basil, *Hexaëmeron*:

> Γενηθήτω φῶς. Καὶ τὸ πρόσταγμα ἔργον ἦν· καὶ φύσις ἐγένετο, ἧς οὐδὲ ἐπινοῆσαί τι τερπνότερον εἰς ἀπόλαυσιν δυνατόν ἐστι λογισμοῖς ἀνθρωπίνοις.[18]

Eustathius:

> Fiat lux, dixit Deus: confestimque praeceptio fuit opus, et facta natura est, quia nihil voluptuosius in fruendo cogitationem poterit subire mortalium.[19]

Grosseteste:

> Et ut ait Basilius: 'Hec est facta natura, qua nichil voluptuosius fruendum cogitacionem potest subire mortalium.'[20]

Symbolica theologia:

> Fiat lux et praeceptum opus fuit et natura generata, qua neque excogitare quid delectabilius in suavitate possibile est mentibus humanis.[21]

Considering on the one hand that the anonymous author is compiling his summary from the works of Robert Grosseteste and Adam Marsh and, on the other, that the present quotation does not come from Grosseteste's *Hexaëmeron,* it may be concluded that the citation of St. Basil in its accurate verbatim style derives from a work by Adam Marsh. If it is unacceptable to say that the friar himself translated his texts from the Greek -- a conclusion that might prove to be true -- one still cannot get away from accepting the fact that, at least, he was very much interested in the original Greek text.

Two more quotations from another Greek Father occur in the summary. Both of them derive from *De fide orthodoxa* of John Damascene, a well known authority who is frequently referred to by Robert Grosseteste.[22] Strictly speaking, just one passage of John Damascene is involved.[23] The first part of it, cited twice in the *Symbolica theologia,*[24] is not found in Grosseteste's *Hexaëmeron*. The fact is the more surprising as the anonymous author, arguing for the effectual beauty of light,[25] transcribes at this point an argument from Grosseteste's work, which consists of a quotation from Augustine and another one from John Damascene. While Augustine's text is copied almost word for word, the citation from John Damascene contains an additional sentence. Unless the author was quoting from a copy of Grosseteste's *Hexaëmeron* with notable variants, he may have borrowed the text from Adam Marsh. Both Grosseteste and the anonymous author use the translation of Burgundio of Pisa.

From the Latin Fathers only Ambrose and Augustine are cited. Ambrose is present with two quotations from his *Hexaëmeron*.[26] The first of them is not among the twenty-one quotations used by Grosseteste in his *Hexaëmeron*.[27] So it may be assumed that the author obtained it from a work of Adam Marsh, particularly since it immediately follows after the word for word translation of a text of Basil which is not found in Grosseteste's work either. The second text, on the contrary, was clearly copied from Grosseteste, as will be seen presently.

St. Augustine is quoted seven times: three citations are from *De Genesi ad litteram*;[28] *De libero arbitrio,* the letter *Ad Volusianum, De musica* and *Confessiones* are each cited only once.[29] All but two of these quotations are present in Grosseteste's *Hexaëmeron.*[30] The first exception regards a definition of beauty explicitly quoted from the sixth book of *De musica* and adduced to confirm the absolute beauty of light in itself. The text would not have been out of place in a marginal note, but is found inserted in a series of sentences almost literally borrowed from Grosseteste. A parallel reproduction of both passages may best illustrate the particular working method of the anonymous author.

Grosseteste, *Hexaëmeron:*	*Symbolica theologia:*
Hec per se pulchra est, quia eius "natura simplex est sibique per omnia similis;" quapropter maxime unita, et ad se per equalitatem concordissime proporcionata. Proporcionum autem concordia pulchritudo est; quapropter eciam sine corporearum figurarum armonica proporcione ipsa lux pulchra est et visui iocundissima.	Absolutam habet lux pulchritudinem ex eo quod sibi est concordantissime, aliis concordissime proportionata. Proportionata namque concordia pulchritudo est.
	Unde Augustinus in sexto *Musicae* dicit, quod pulchritudo est aequalitas numerosa.
Unde et aurum sine decore figurarum ex rutilanti fulgore pulchrum est; et stelle visui apparent pulcherrime, cum nullum tamen ostendant nobis decorem ex membrorum compaginacione aut figurarum proporcione, sed ex solo luminis fulgore.	Hinc est quod aurum ex rutilanti fulgore pulchrum est, etiam absque decore cuiuslibet figurae, propter absolutam lucis pulchritudinem.
Ut enim dicit Ambrosius: "Lucis natura huiusmodi est, ut non in numero, non in mensura, non in pondere ut alia, sed omnis eius in aspectu gracia sit; ipsaque facit, ut eciam cetera membra mundi digna sint laudibus."[31]	Hinc est quod dicit Ambrosius: "Lucis natura huiusmodi est, ut non in numero, non in mensura, non in pondere ut alia, sed omnis eius in aspectu gratia sit. Ipsaque facit, ut cetera membra mundi digna sint laudibus."[32]

Still a last quotation deserves attention. It occurs in section 4.2.1 on light, according to its operation, and relative to things existing in the divine mind. Having reassumed in one sentence the famous chapter of Grosseteste's *Hexaëmeron,* where the union of the three divine persons is exemplified by the nature of light,[33] the anonymous author cites an "unbelieving philosopher" saying that "God is pervious light which does not brighten by refraction."[34] The maxim is written, he claims, in the definitions of the twenty-four philosophers. He also explains the meaning of the rather obscure saying: when material light falls upon a body of matter so obscure that it cannot purge it or go through it, it is broken up in rays and from this refraction of rays it shines. But since the divine light cannot be withstood, it is not broken, but in its vigorous clarity goes unremittingly through all things.

The definitions of the twenty-four philosophers to which the author refers is a modest pseudo-hermetic treatise of the twelfth century. It is generally quoted as *Liber XXIV philosophorum,* but in the manuscript it is called *Liber de propositionibus sive regulis theologiae, qui dicitur Termegisti Philosophi.* It contains a series of twenty-four maxims, or rather definitions, regarding God. All of them start with the wording "Deus est . . .," and are followed by a short comment. Clemens Baeumker published the treatise from the manuscripts, together with an excellent introduction.[35] At this point, having identified the work and a modern edition, it is disappointing to find that the definition, in the form it is quoted by the anonymous author, does not appear in Baeumker's edition. Is that to say that it does not belong to it? That is unlikely. It seems quite possible, and it is almost certain, that the summary preserves the original version of definition 24. In Baeumker's edition this maxim reads: "Deus est, qui sola ignorantia mente cognoscitur";[36] but in the footnotes the editor honestly remarks that in two of the three extant manuscripts the sentence is missing. In the third manuscript it is preceded by the words *Vel sic*, regarded as superfluous by the editor and consigned to the footnotes. Yet, the comment that follows, however confused, is exactly what one would expect if the author were explaining the maxim as quoted in the *Symbolica theologia*. Therefore it may be presumed that the original sentence read: "Deus est lux pervia, quae fractione non clarescit," and that it afterwards was enlarged by the alternative adage: "Vel sic: Deus est, qui sola ignorantia mente cognoscitur."

As to the comment, the medieval author of the summary doubtless produces a more sensible explanation of the twenty-fourth definition than Clemens Baeumker was able to reconstruct from his corrupt manuscripts. His text is as follows:

> XXIV. *Deus est, qui sola ignorantia mente cognoscitur.*
>
> Haec definitio est ad essentiam data. Lux creata, cum cadit super rem tenebrosam tantae tenebrositatis, ita quod non sit potens lux illa purgare tenebrosum propter sui vehementum possibilitatem, tunc frangitur lux in radiis, et sic, cum sit in maxime se multiplicantibus, pertransit illud densum medium. Contraria infinitum in ipsis creaturis respectu lucis divinae. Cum enim non sit

tanta possibilitas in rebus creatis, quae frangat lucem divinam in sui actione, immo omnia pertransit. Sed cum sit in re aliqua deformitas, scilicet respectu sui creatoris, tunc in illa claritatem aliquam generat, in se vero nullam. Et sic intelligentia creata sola ignorantia mente cognoscitur.[37]

Compare this with the text as found in the *Symbolica theologia*:

Et de Deo dicat philosophus incredulus: "Deus est lux pervia, quae fractione non clarescit." Hoc habetur in *Diffinitionibus XXIIIIor philosophorum*. Et ratio dicti videtur, quia lux materialis, cadens super corpus aliquod ita obscurum quod illud purgare sive pertransire non potest, frangitur in radiis, et ex tali radiorum refractione clarescit. Lux autem divina, quia nullum potest habere resistentiam, non frangitur, sed in suae claritatis vigore per omnia iremissibiliter transit.[38]

As far as is known, in his authentic writings Robert Grosseteste does not quote from the *Liber XXIV philosophorum*, neither explicitly nor implicitly. Should it, in that case, again be concluded that the quotation from the incredulous philosopher, with its plain comment, comes from a work by Adam Marsh? If so, the doubtless remarkable text could possibly give support to Roger Bacon's assertion that Adam through the power of mathematics (read: light-metaphysics) was able to explain the causes of all things, both human and divine.[39]

Robert Grosseteste and Adam Marsh

In an otherwise excellent contribution on St. Bonaventure, Ephrem Longpré suggests that the Seraphic Doctor had studied a treatise *De luce*, composed by Adam Marsh.[40] For his evidence he gave a general reference to the unpublished *Symbolica theologia*.[41] Unfortunately, there is nothing in this pseudo-Bonaventurian work to justify his affirmation. As has been seen here, the anonymous author collected a number of pronouncements on light according as he had found them introduced "in the writings" of Robert Grosseteste and Adam Marsh. He did not specify which writings of either he copied. So far as Grosseteste is concerned, the problem can easily be solved. The anonymous author used almost exclusively chapter ten of the second part of Grosseteste's *Hexaëmeron*.[42] In the footnotes to the edition of the summary on light (see the Appendix) are reproduced the exact texts. Generally speaking it may be noticed that the literal or nearly literal quotations from Grosseteste's *Hexaëmeron* occupy more than half of the summary. If, relying on the authority of the anonymous informant, the remaining text is attributed to Adam Marsh, it is possible to trace the following diagram of parts belonging to each of them:

Symbolica theologia	Grosseteste	Adam Marsh
Introduction		0
Light as substance:		
noble		1.1
substantial	1.2	
subtle	1.3	
Light as virtue:		
multipliable	2.1	
inflectible		2.2
incoercible		2.3
Light as appearance:		
beautiful	3.1	3.1 (partially)
causing beauty	3.2	
remaining beautiful	3.3	
Light as operation:		
in itself		
is and transmits	4.1.1	
transmits and diffuses		4.1.2
diffuses and brightens	4.1.3	
its properties		
not refusing		4.1.4.1
manifesting	4.1.4.2	
distinguishing		4.1.4.3
relative to other beings		
divine mind	4.2.1	4.2.1 (mostly)
dwelling of blessed		4.2.2
universe		
man		
soul		4.2.3.1.1
body	4.2.3.1.2	4.2.3.1.2 (partially)
conjunction		4.2.3.1.3
world		
beyond heaven		4.2.3.2.1
celestial region		4.2.3.2.2
beneath heaven	4.2.3.2.3	4.2.3.2.3 (partially)

From the structure of this survey and from what has been discussed before, one conclusion emerges with great evidence. If the summary on light, as its author asserts, was indeed drawn from the writings of both Grosseteste and Adam Marsh, these two scholars and friends perfectly concorded, not only in pastoral and political affairs as is commonly agreed, but also in their basic doctrinal methods and beliefs. It would not be possible to construct so coherent a synthesis on light by piecing together tenets of authors who were not profoundly congenial thinkers. Probably Roger Bacon was right when he so often pronounced the names of Grosseteste and Adam Marsh in the same breath.

Notes

[1] On Adam Marsh, see A. B. Emden, *A Bibliographical Register of the University of Oxford to A.D. 1500* (Oxford, 1958), 2:1225-6, with bibliography; for his relations with Grosseteste: Fr. Cuthbert (Hess), "Adam Marsh: An English Franciscan of the Thirteenth Century," in id., *The Romanticism of St. Francis and Other Studies in the Genius of the Franciscans* (London, 1924), pp. 190-235. His correspondence, edited by J. S. Brewer, is contained in *Monumenta Franciscana* (London, 1858), 2:77-489; Grosseteste's letters are published by H. Luard, *Roberti Grosseteste Epistolae*, London, 1861.

[2] Cf. *Opus tertium*, chap. 25: "Nam omnes sancti et philosophi Latini et poetae sciverunt de linguis alienis, et omnes sapientes antiqui, quorum multos vidimus durare usque ad nostrum tempus; ut dominos episcopum Lincolniensem et Sancti David et fratrem Adam et multos viros," ed. Brewer (London, 1859), p. 88, with the corrections by A. G. Little in *Archivum Fratrum Minorum* 19 (1926), p. 811 n. 5; *Opus maius*: "Nam vidimus aliquos de antiquis qui laboraverunt multum in linguis, sicut fuit Dominus Robertus praefatus translator et episcopus, et Thomas venerabilis antistes Sancti David nuper defunctus, et frater Adam de Marisco," ed. Bridges (London, 1900), 3:88.

[3] Cf. *Opus maius*: "Inventi enim sunt viri famosissimi, ut Episcopus Robertus Lincolniensis, et Frater Adam de Marisco, et multi alii, qui per potestatem mathematicae sciverunt causas omnium explicare, et tam humana quam divina sufficienter exponere. Hujus autem rei certitudo patet in scriptis illorum virorum, ut de impressionibus, sicut de iride et de cometis, et de generatione caloris, et locorum mundi investigatione, et de coelestibus et aliis, quibus tam theologia quam philosophia utitur," ed. Bridges (Oxford, 1897), 1:108; *De communibus mathematice*: "Nullus potest pervenire ad noticiam illius sciencie secundum modum vulgatum nisi cum ponat 30 vel 40 annos, ut planum est in eis qui floruerunt in hiis scienciis, sicut Dominus Robertus felicis memorie nuper episcopus Lincolniensis ecclesie, et Frater Adam de Marisco, et Magister Johannes Londoniensis," Oxford, Bodleian Library, MS Digby 76, fol. 56va, quoted by D. E. Smith, *Roger Bacon: Essays* (Oxford, 1914), p. 164 n. 2.

[4] This is the opinion of A. G. Little in his authoritative study "The Franciscan School at Oxford in the Thirteenth Century," *Archivum Franciscanum Historicum* 19 (1929), 803-74, in particular p. 836.

[5] Servus (Gieben) of Sint Anthonis, "The Pseudo-Bonaventurian Work 'Symbolica theologia,' with the Edition of its Table of Contents and Some Extracts," *Miscellanea Melchor de Pobladura* (Rome, 1964), 1:173-95. On pp. 182-83 I called attention to this passage. See B. Distelbrink, *Bonaventurae scripta, authentica, dubia vel spuria, critice recensita* (Rome, 1975), pp. 199-200 n. 224.

[6] "Quinta distinctio, de signis significantibus angelicam dignitatem. Et habet capitula XIX . . . Capitulum nonum. Quomodo angelis conveniant naturales proprietates lucis." The chapter is preserved only in the Toulouse manuscript (Bibliothèque de la Ville 232, fols. 61v-63r), not in the mutilated Basel copy (Universitätsbibliothek A. VI. 34).

[7] For this and other quotations I refer the reader to the Latin text, published at the end of the article.

[8] Cf. Robert Grosseteste, *Hexaëmeron*, ed. Richard C. Dales and Servus Gieben, Auctores Britannici Medii Aevi 6 (London, 1982), pp. 97-100.

[9] The end of this work significantly reads: "Explicit libellus introductorius ad figurativas locutiones divinarum Scripturarum" (fol. 86v).

[10] R. W. Hunt discussed Adam Marsh's fondness for summaries in *The Bodleian Library Record* 4 (1953), 244-46 and 5 (1954), 63-68. In the latter contribution, "Chapter Headings of Augustine 'De Trinitate' ascribed to Adam Marsh," the summaries are proved to be erroneously attributed to Adam. Genuine summaries or chapter headings by Adam Marsh, or at least using his formula, can be found in Cambridge, St. John's College, MSS 17 and 47 (works by Augustine and Anselm); in

Oxford, Bodleian Library, MS Lat. th. e. 39 (Augustine, *De doctrina Christiana*); in Robert Grosseteste, *Hexaëmeron*, ed. Dales and Gieben, pp. 341-50; in Thomas of York, *Sapientiale*, ed. of the chapter summaries in *Archivum Franciscanum Historicum* 19 (1926), pp. 906-29.

[11] "Sermo in ponendis naturalibus lucis proprietatibus quibus intelligi valeant eciam proprietates rerum mistice signatarum, et sunt 20 modi quos ponit." Cf. Grosseteste, *Hexaëmeron*, p. 343.

[12] For the sake of clarity I have numbered the divisions and added the essential Latin words between brackets.

[13] *Hexaëmeron*, p. 93 (Gen. 1.4), p. 96 (Eph. 5.13), p. 177 (John 8.12).

[14] There are ninety-three citations from it in Grosseteste's *Hexaëmeron*. Grosseteste possessed a copy of the book which he had exchanged for another work with the monks of Bury St. Edmunds. Cf. Grosseteste, *Hexaëmeron*, pp. xxii and xxiv-xxv.

[15] PG 29:48.

[16] *Eustathii hexaemeri metaphrasis* 2.7 (PG 30:890).

[17] See the summary, included as an appendix to this article, 0.1.

[18] PG 29:45.

[19] *Eustathii hexaemeri metaphrasis* 2.7 (PG 30:889).

[20] Grosseteste, *Hexaëmeron* 2.10.4 (p. 99).

[21] See the summary 4.2.3.1.1.

[22] *De fide orthodoxa* is quoted seventeen times in Grosseteste's *Hexaëmeron*; see p. xxii. He apparently used the translation of Burgundio of Pisa, though sometimes in a tradition not recorded by the modern editor: Saint John Damascene, *De fide orthodoxa, Versions of Burgundio and Cerbanus*, ed. Eligius M. Buytaert (St. Bonaventure, New York, 1955).

[23] *De fide orthodoxa* 21.1 (ed. Buytaert, p. 84).

[24] See the summary 1.1 and 3.2.

[25] Ibid. 3.2.

[26] Ibid. 0.1 and 3.1.

[27] Cf. Grosseteste, *Hexaëmeron*, p. xx.

[28] See the summary 1.3, 3.2 and 4.2.3.1.2 (twice).

[29] Ibid. 1.2 (*De libero arbitrio* and *Ad Volusianum*), 3.1 (*De musica*).

[30] Grosseteste, *Hexaëmeron* 2.10.2 (pp. 98-99).

[31] Ibid. 2.10.4 (pp. 99-100).

[32] See the summary 3.1.

[33] *Hexaëmeron* 8.3 (pp. 220-22). See also pp. 100, 223.

[34] See the summary 4.2.1.

[35] Clemens Baeumker, *Das pseudo-hermetische "Buch der vierundzwanzig Meister" (Liber XXIV philosophorum): ein Beitrag zur Geschichte des Neupythagoreismus und Neuplatonismus im Mittelalter*, Studien und Charakteristiken zur Geschichte der Philosophie, insbesondere des Mittelalters: gesammelte Vorträge, ed. M. Grabmann (Münster i. W., 1927), pp. 194-214. The *Liber XXIV philosophorum* is edited on pp. 207-14. The edition was characterized by Grabmann as "ein Kabinettstück feinsinniger ideengeschichtlicher Untersuchung und vollendeter Editionstechnik" (p. 28).

[35] Ibid., p. 214.

[37] Ibid., p. 214.

[38] See the summary 4.2.1.

[39] See the text quoted in n. 3.

[40] E. Longpré, "Bonaventure (Saint)," in *Dictionnaire d'histoire et de géographie ecclésiastiques* (Paris, 1937), 9:741-88, particularly col. 746.

[41] When I was working on this article, a French student paid me a visit to discuss some questions regarding the edition of the *Symbolica theologia*, which he was preparing for print. Hopefully the book will be published in the near future.

[42] Ed. Dales, pp. 97-100.

Appendix

Toulouse, Bibliothèque de la Ville, MS 232, fols. 61v-63r
[*Symbolica theologia*, distinctio quinta]
[fol. 61v] *Capitulum nonum. Quomodo angelis conveniant naturales proprietates lucis*

01 De luce vero scriptum est: *Vidit Deus lucem quod esset bona.*[1] Super hoc verbo Basilius in *Exameron*: [62r] "Dei iudicium de bono non omnino ad illud quod in visu delectabile respicientis sed ad eam quae in posterum ab ipsa utilitatem praevidentis factum est."[2] Ambrosius in *Exameron*: "Non in splendore tantummodo, sed in omnium utilitate gratia lucis probatur."[3] Haec Ambrosius. Huius autem bonitas est usus bonus ipsius et utilitas quam in mundo suis proprietatibus naturalibus operatur. Ut ergo materialis lucis proprietates ad angelos transferre possimus, quos per lucem significari diximus, ipsarum proprietates assignare curabo aliquas, prout a magnis doctoribus, scilicet episcopo Lincolniensi et fratre Adam de Marisco, in eorum scriptis reperi introductas.

Potest ergo considerari lux corporalis quadrupliciter: vel secundum substantiam, vel secundum virtutem, vel secundum speciem, vel secundum operationem.

1 Lux secundum substantiam est origine nobilis, quiditate substantialis, essentia subtilis.

1.1 Origine nobilis, quoniam divinorum operum opus primogenitum. Unde Johannes Damascenus, libro 2°, capitulo XXIIII°: "In principio quidem fecit Deus lumen scilicet prima die."[4]

1.2 Quiditate substantialis, quoniam substantia corporea in suo scilicet fonte concrete considerata. Unde[5] Augustinus 3° *De libero arbitrio* dicit, lucem in corporalibus primum locum tenere.[6] Idem epistola *Ad Volusianum,* loquens de vano quorundam intellectu de Deo, dicit: "Hominum iste sensus est nichil nisi corpora valentium cogitare, sive ista crassiora sunt sicut humor atque humus, sive subtiliora sicut aeris et lucis, sed tamen corpora."[7] Haec Augustinus. Lucem vocat ignem; quod patet, quia nominat ibi quatuor elementa. Unde[8] lux est substantia subtilissima et incorporalitate proxima. Significat tamen nichilominus quandam accidentalem qualitatem de generativa sua naturali actione procedentem.

Ipsa enim generativae actionis indeficiens motio qualitas est substantiae sese generantis.

1.3 Et ex hoc sequitur tertia proprietas, essentia videlicet subtilis quia simplex; quoniam[9] secundum Augustinum *Super Genesim ad litteram*, libro XII°: Id quod in natura corporea est subtilissimum, et ob hoc animae quae est simplex et incorporea maxime vicinum, est lux.[10] Eius[11] quippe natura vere simplex est, quoniam sibi per omnia similis est et ad se per aequalitatem concordissime proportionata.

2 Lux etiam secundum virtutem est multiplicabilis, inflexibilis, incoarctabilis.

2.1 Multiplicabilis[12] est, immo sui ipsius generativa undique. Simul enim est et generat. Unde subito replet locum undique circumstantem, cum lux subito genita simul gignitur, est et gignit lucem sibi proximo succedentem, et ita consequenter. Et talis generatio est sui manifestatio.[13] Non enim est aliquid aliud per quod lux habeat fieri manifesta, sed ipsa se et alia manifestat per generativam sui virtutem.[14]

2.2 Inflexibilis est, quia habet incessum rectum et nullo modo curvabilem.[15] Frangi namque potest lucis radius et reflecti, sed nequaquam curvari.[16] Et huius reflectio seu fractio est sui multiplicativa.

2.3 Incoarctabilis est, quia non potest includi. Si enim claudere fenestram volueris, lucem non includes sed excludes. Non enim potest lux ipsa a suo fonte discontinuari.

3 Lux est secundum speciem in se absolute pulchra, in pulchris effective pulchra, in foedis mansive pulchra.

3.1 Absolutam[17] habet lux pulchritudinem ex eo quod sibi est concordantissime, aliis concordissime proportionata. Proportionata namque concordia pulchritudo est. Unde Augustinus in sexto *Musicae* dicit, quod pulchritudo est aequalitas numerosa.[18] Hinc est quod aurum ex rutilanti fulgore pulchrum est, etiam absque decore cuiuslibet figurae, propter absolutam lucis pulchritudinem. Hinc est quod dicit Ambrosius: "Lucis natura huiusmodi est, ut non in numero, non in mensura, non in pondere ut alia, sed omnino eius in aspectu grata sit. Ipsaque facit, ut cetera membra mundi digna sint laudibus."[19] Et ex hoc sequitur secundum, scilicet:

3.2 Quod in pulchris est effective pulchra. Sine luce namque nullius rei pulchritudo apparet, sed lux omnia pulchrificat. Unde[20] dicitur ab Augustino colorum regina,[21] utpote eorundem per incorporationem effectiva et per superfusionem motiva. Lux namque incorporata in perspicuo humido color est; qui color sui speciem per se in aere generare non potest propter incorporationis retardationem. Sed lux superfusa colori movet eum in actum generationis suae speciei. Sine luce ergo omnia sunt ignota. Unde Johannes Damascenus: "In principio quidem fecit Deus lumen scilicet prima die pulchritudinem et ornatam omnis visibilis creaturae. Aufer lumen, et omnia in tenebris ignota manebunt, proprium cum non possint demonstrare decorem."[22]

3.3 Est 3° lux in foedis mansive pulchra. Haec[23] enim radios suos de mundi luminaribus ad terram usque protendit, et tamen radii eius per quaeque immunda diffusi non contaminantur.

4 Lux tandem secundum operationem potest considerari absolute in se et relata ad esse rerum.

4.1 Lux ergo secundum operationem absolutam est: ut simul sit et gignat, simul gignat et se diffundat, simul se diffundat et clarescat.

4.1.1 Simul ergo[24] lux est et generat, quoniam ipsius actio naturalis est ei inseparabilis, et similis, et irretardabilis; propter quod statim cum est lucet, cum suo esse generat lucem; et hoc tactum est supra,[25] ubi ostensum est lucem secundum virtutem esse multiplicabilem.

4.1.2 Item simul gignit et se circumfundit. Cum enim per omnia sit sibi similis, si ex una, et ex omni parte se circumfundit [62v] ubi obiectum aliquod densum non impendit. Si enim inveniat corpus densum, cum non possit se diffundere in directum, diffundit se ad partem oppositum reflectendo ad angulos aequales angulis incidentiae. Radius enim directe incidens directe reflectitur, et incidens oblique ad parem reflectitur obliquitatem.

4.1.3 Tertio, lux simul se diffundit et clarescit, quoniam circumfusa simul est luci originanti; et ideo[26] lux prior secundum locum generat lucem sequentem; et lux genita, ut dictum est supra,[27] simul gignitur et est et gignit, et sic consequenter. Et ita unus punctus lucis posset orbem totum replere lumine si non inveniret corpus densum sibi oppositum.

4.1.4 Lux iterum hoc habet proprium, ut nulli se neget, omnia manifestet, et singula distinguat.

4.1.4.1 Nulli se negat, quia latere non potest. Sola enim est quae non potest includi nisi exclusa, sicut patet in obseratione fenestrae.[28]

4.1.4.2 Item omnia manifestat. Unde[29] Apostolus, Ephes. V°: *Omne quod manifestatur lumen est*.[30]

4.1.4.3 Ultimo, singula distinguendo designat. Est enim omnium sensibilium differentiarum distinctiva. Est enim, sicut dictum est supra,[31] de effectu pulchrificandi pulchra. Lux movet omnem colorem in actum generationis speciei propriae, ita quod omnis creatura corporalis gignit radiose suam speciem ex se ipsa, licet secundum disparem efficaciam. In quantum ergo lux est specierum huius delativa, in tantum est omnium distinctiva.[32] Unde et visus, cui proprie lux deservit, cuilibet sensui adaptatur. Ita ut dicamus: vide, sive sit in aspectu coloratum, sive in auditu grave vel acutum, sive in olfatu redolens aut foetidum, sive in gestu dulce vel amarum, sive in tactu molle vel durum.

4.2 Lux quoque secundum operationem relatam potest considerari: vel ut habet comparationem ad res existentes in mente divina, vel ut habet comparationem ad habitationem beatorum creatam, vel ut habet comparationem ad mundi machinam universam.

4.2.1 Lux ergo secundum comparationem ad artem divinam est illius nobilissimum vestigium et illius mundi archetipi demonstratio manifesta;[33] ita ut dicat Dei filius qui est ars omnium rationum viventium: *Ego sum lux mundi*, Jo. VIII°.[34] Et de Deo dicat philosophus incredulus:[35] "Deus est lux pervia, quae fractione non clarescit." Hoc habetur in *Diffinitionibus XXIIIIor philosophorum.*[36] Et ratio dicti videtur, quia lux materialis, cadens super corpus aliquod ita obscurum quod illud purgare sive pertransire non potest, frangitur in radiis, et ex tali radiorum refractione clarescit. Lux autem divina, quia nullam potest habere resistentiam, non frangitur, sed in suae claritatis vigore per omnia iremissibiliter transit. Dicit etiam divinus theologus, prima Jo. 1°: Deus lux est et tenebrae in eo non sunt ullae.[37]

4.2.2 Secundum comparationem ad habitationem beatorum creatam, lux est eorum habitatio convenientissima,[38] de qua dicit Apostolus, [ad] Hebreos, XI°: Expectabat fundamenta habentem civitatem, cuius artifex et conditor Deus;[39] dicitur de Abraam. De cuius refulgentia Apocal. XXI°: *Civitas non eget sole neque luna ut luceant in ea.*[40]

4.2.3 Porro, secundum comparationem quam habet lux ad mundi machinam universam, in eo operatur secundum luminaria, maius scilicet et minus, et stellas. Unde notandum, quod lux in universo habet comparari ad minorem et maiorem mundum. Minor mundus est homo, maior vero universa moles mundialis.

4.2.3.1 In homo ergo est anima, corpus, et compositum.

4.2.3.1.1 Quantum ad animam, lux in rebus corporalibus est iocundissima apprehensio.[41] Unde[42] Basilius: "Fiat lux et praeceptum opus fuit et natura generata, qua neque excogitare quid delectabilius in suavitate possibile est mentibus humanis."[43] Cuius est signum quod sublimissimo sensuum est summe iocunda. Unde: *Dulce lumen et delectabile est oculis videre solem.* Eccles. XI°.[44]

4.2.3.1.2 Quantum ad corpus,[45] est instrumentum primum animae in omni actione sensitiva, sicut dicit Augustinus, libro XII° *Super Genesi ad litteram*: Illud autem quod est subtilissimum in corpore, et ob hoc animae vicinius quam caetera, est lux.

"Primum per oculos sola diffunditur emicatque in radiis oculorum ad visibilia contuenda. Deinde mixtura quadam, primo cum aere puro, secundo cum aere caliginoso atque nebuloso, tertio cum corpulentiore humore, quarto cum terrena crassitudine, quinque sensus cum ipso ubi sola excellit oculorum sensu efficit."[46] Idem iterum, libro septimo, circa medium: "Anima," inquit, "quoniam res est incorporea, corpus quod incorporeo vicinum est, sicuti est ignis vel potius lux et etiam aer, primitus agit et per hoc caetera quae crassiora sunt corporis, sicuti humor et terra -- unde carnis corpulentia solidatur -- quae magis sunt ad patiendum subdita quam praedita ad agendum."[47]

4.2.3.1.3 Quantum ad coniunctum, est naturarum tam distantium unitiva, quoniam, secundum philosophos naturales,[48] lux quaedam caelestis est illud quod medici vocant spiritum,[49] quod est intra corpus et animam medium unionis alterius actionis.

4.2.3.2 Lux tandem in maiori mundo, scilicet in tota mole mundiali, potest comparari ad regionem supracaelestem, caelestem et subcaelestem.

4.2.3.2.1 In regione supracaelesti, ubi est mundus incorruptibilis et invisibilis nobis, lux totum perficit et replet sine alio corpore replente. Et illud dicimus caelum empyreum.

4.2.3.2.2 In regione caelesti, ubi est mundus in se incorruptibilis et nobis visibilis, lux ornat, sicut apparet in luminaribus. Et istud dicimus firmamentum. [63r]

4.2.3.2.3 In regione vero subcaelesti, ubi est mundus in se corruptibilis et visibilis ac sensibilis nobis, lux purgat tenebras, subtiliat crassitudinem, et donat fertilitatem.

Quapropter,[50] cum lux tantae dignitatis sit, merito Deus, qui lux est inaccessibilis, a luce sex dierum opera inchoavit, quando dixit Deus: *Fiat lux et facta est lux.*

Hae lucis corporalis proprietates tactae sunt, ut ex eis studiosioribus et perspicatioribus detur materia et excogitandi alias et eas ad angelicam dignitatem necnon ad alios sensus mysticos transferendi.

Notes

[1] Gen. 1.4. Cf. Robert Grosseteste, *Hexaëmeron*, ed. Richard C. Dales and Servus Gieben, Auctores Britannici Medii Aevi 6 (London, 1982), p. 93.

[2] Basil of Caesarea, *Hexaemeron* 2.7 (PG 29:48); trans. Eustathius, *Eustathii hexaemeri metaphrasis* 2.7 (PG 30:890). See discussion in main article, pp. 19-21.

[3] Ambrose, *Hexaemeron* 1.9.34 (PL 14:154); instead of *omnium*, the printed text reads *omni*.

[4] John Damascene, *De fide orthodoxa* 2.7 (PG 94:888); *De fide orthodoxa, Versions of Burgundio and Cerbanus*, ed. Eligius M. Buytaert (St. Bonaventure, New York, 1955), p. 84.

[5] For this passage, see Grosseteste, *Hexaëmeron* 2.10.1: "Hec, secundum Augustinum in libro II *De libero arbitrio*, corpus est et in corporibus primum tenet locum. In epistola quoque *Ad Volusianum* idem Augustinus, loquens de vano quorundam intellectu de Deo, sic ait: 'Hominum iste sensus est nichil nisi corpora valencium cogitare sive ista crassiora, sicut sunt humor atque humus, sive subtiliora sicut aeris et lucis, sed tamen corpora'" (p. 98).

[6] Cf. Augustine, *De libero arbitrio* 3.15.16 (PL 32:1279).

[7] Augustine, *Epistola CXXXVII* 2.4 (PL 33:517).

[8] See Grosseteste, *Hexaëmeron* 2.10.2: "signat enim substanciam corpoream subtilissimam et incorporalitati proximam, naturaliter sui ipsius generativam; et significat accidentalem qualitatem, de lucis substancie naturali generativa accione procedentem. Ipsa enim generative accionis indeficiens mocio qualitas est substancie indeficienter sese generantis" (pp. 98-99).

[9] See Grosseteste, *Hexaëmeron* 2.10.1: "Lux quoque secundum Augustinum est id quod in natura corporea est subtilissimum; et ob hoc anime, que simpliciter incorporea est, maxime vicinum" (p. 98).

[10] Augustine, *De Genesi ad litteram* 12.16.32 (PL 34:466).

[11] See Grosseteste, *Hexaëmeron* 2.10.4: "quia eius 'natura simplex est sibique per omnia similis'; quapropter maxime unita, et ad se per equalitatem concordissime proporcionata" (p. 99). See also Basil, *Hexaemeron* 2.7 (PG 29:48; transl. Eustathius PG 30:889).

[12] See Grosseteste, *Hexaëmeron* 2.10.1: "Est itaque lux sui ipsius naturaliter undique multiplicativa, et, ut ita dicam, generativitas quaedam sui ipsius quodammodo de sui substancia. Naturaliter enim lux undique se multiplicat gignendo, et simul cum est generat. Quapropter replet circumstantem locum subito; lux enim prior secundum locum gignit lucem sequentem; et lux genita simul gignitur et est et gignit lucem sibi proximo succedentem; et illa succedens adhuc succedentem ulterius; et ita consequenter" (p. 97).

[13] See Grosseteste, *Hexaëmeron* 2.10.1: "Et forte inde quod lux est naturaliter sui generativa, est eciam sui manifestativa, quia forte sui generativitas ipsa manifestabilitas est" (p. 98).

[14] On light as a manifestation "vel manifestans, vel manifestata, vel cui manifestatur," see Grosseteste's *Dictum* 55, "Dedi te in lucem gentium" (Cambridge, MS Caius 380+/380, fols. 51v-52ra).

[15] See Grosseteste, *Hexaëmeron* 2.10.4: "Hec directum habet incessum, et nullo modo incedit per curvum" (p. 100).

[16] See Grosseteste, *Hexaëmeron* 2.10.4: "Lux quoque ad corporum politorum superficies in angulis reflectitur equalibus" (p. 100).

[17] For this passage, see the comment in the main article, p. 22.

[18] Cf. Augustine, *De musica* 6.13.38: "An aliud quam aequalitatem numerosam esse arbitraris . . .?" (PL 32:1184).

[19] Ambrose, *Hexaemeron* 1.9.34 (PL 14:154).

[20] See Grosseteste, *Hexaëmeron* 2.10.2: "Est quoque lux, ut dicit Augustinus, colorum regina, utpote eorumdem per incorporacionem effectiva et per superfusionem motiva. Lux namque incorporata in perspicuo humido color est; qui color sui speciem in aere propter incorporacionis sue retardacionem per se generare non potest; sed lux colori superfusa movet eum in generacionis sue speciei actum. Sine luce itaque omnia corporea occulta sunt et ignota. Unde Iohannes Damascenus ait: 'Aufer lumen et omnia in tenebris ignota manebunt, cum non possint proprium demonstrare decorem'" (p. 99).

[21] Augustine, *Confessiones* 10.34.51 (PL 32:800).

[22] John Damascene, *De fide orthodoxa* 2.7 (PG 94:888; ed. Buytaert, p. 84).

[23] See Grosseteste, *Hexaëmeron* 2.10.4: "Hec, ut dicit Augustinus, cum de mundi luminaribus radios suos terras usque pertendat, tamen eius radii per queque immunda diffusi non contaminantur" (p. 100).

[24] See passage from Grosseteste's *Hexaëmeron* in note 12.

[25] That is, in 2.1.

[26] See Grosseteste, *Hexaëmeron* 2.10.1: "lux enim prior secundum locum gignit lucem sequentem; et lux genita simul gignitur et est et gignit lucem sibi proximo succedentem; et illa succedens adhuc succedentem ulterius; et ita consequenter. Unde in instanti uno unus lucis punctus replere potest orbem lumine" (pp. 97-98).

[27] See 2.1.

[28] See 2.3.

[29] See Grosseteste, *Hexaëmeron* 2.8.2: "Omnis namque forma quedam lux est et manifestacio materie quam informat, ut ait Paulus: *Omne quod manifestatur lux est*" (p. 96).

[30] Ephes. 5.13.

[31] See 3.2.

[32] See Grosseteste, *Hexaëmeron* 2.10.4: "omniumque corporalium formas et ymagines ubique representat, et quod in uno loco est per substanciam in omni loco dinumerat et collocat per ymaginem et formam" (p. 100).

[33] See Grosseteste, *Hexaëmeron* 2.10.4: "hec in rebus corporalibus summe Trinitatis per exemplum demonstracio manifestissima" (p. 100); 8.4.7: "Inter res autem corporeas manifestissimum Trinitatis exemplum est ignis, sive lux, quae necessario de se gignit splendorem; et hec duo in se reflectunt mutuum fervorem" (p. 223); and especially 8.3.1 (p. 220).

[34] John 8.12.

[35] See the comment in the article, pp. 23-24.

[36] *Liber XXIV philosophorum* 24, Clemens Baeumker, *Das pseudo-hermetische "Buch der vierundzwanzig Meister" (Liber XXIV philosophorum): ein Beitrag zur Geschichte des Neupythagoreismus und Neuplatonismus im Mittelalter*, Studien und Charakteristiken zur Geschichte der Philosophie, insbesondere des Mittelalters: gesammelte Vorträge, ed. M. Grabmann (Münster i. W., 1927), p. 214.

[37] 1 John 1.5.

[38] See Grosseteste, *Hexaëmeron* 2.10.4: "Hec est angelorum et sanctorum, ut testatur Basilius, supra celum primum diffusa habitacio quietissima" (p. 100).

[39] Hebr. 11.10.

[40] Apoc. 21.23.

[41] Cf. Grosseteste, *Hexaëmeron* 2.10.4: "quapropter eciam sine corporearum figurarum armonica proporcione ipsa lux pulchra est et visui iocundissima" (p. 99).

[42] On this passage, see the comment in the article on p. 21.

[43] Basil, *Hexaemeron* 2.7 (PG 29:45; transl. Eustathius PG 30:889).

[44] Eccles. 11.7.

[45] See Grosseteste, *Hexaëmeron* 2.10.1: "Et ideo est ipsi anime in agendo per corpus velud instrumentum primum, per quod instrumentum primo motum movet cetera corpulenciora. Lux itaque instrumentalis anime in sentiendo per sensus corporeos 'primum per oculos sola et pura diffunditur emicatque in radiis ad visibilia contuenda, deinde mixtura quadam primo cum aere puro, secundo cum aere caliginoso atque nebuloso, tercio cum corpulenciore humore, quarto cum terrena crassitudine, quinque sensus cum ipso ubi sola excellit oculorum sensu efficit'" (p. 98).

[46] Augustine, *De Genesi ad litteram* 12.16.32 (PL 34:466).

[47] Ibid. 7.15.21 (PL 34:363). In the printed text the last word reads *faciendum*, not *agendum*.

[48] On this question, see e.g. Alfred of Sareshel (Alfredus Anglicus), *De motu cordis* 10: *De spiritu*, ed. C. Baeumker (Münster i. W., 1923), pp. 37-45.

[49] The MS reads *speciem.*

[50] See Grosseteste, *Hexaëmeron* 2.10.4: "Quapropter Deus, qui lux est, ab ipsa luce cuius tanta est dignitas merito inchoavit sex dierum opera" (p. 100).

Grosseteste on the Soul's Care for the Body: A New Text and New Sources for the Idea

James McEvoy

Robert Grosseteste appears to have been alone among medieval theologians in arguing that the wounds inflicted on Christ during the relatively short hours of his passion and crucifixion were not of themselves sufficient to cause his death. Rather, his sacrifice of his life on the cross consisted of the voluntary sundering of his soul from his body, a separation which entailed infinite suffering, because so long as the body is not vanquished by its own inherent tendency to material dissolution, no finite power is sufficient to cancel the natural care of the soul for the body which it vivifies.

No source for this thesis of Grosseteste, taken in its entirety, has yet been found, nor is there any known evidence which would suggest that his idea was taken up by later thinkers of the Middle Ages.[1] But one never knows what remains to be uncovered in unedited sources. That is why among the most useful contributions to historical studies are those which attempt to offer clear outlines of ideas and justifiable hints as to their sources. In the recent research on Grosseteste's thought, Richard C. Dales has made a remarkable contribution to the filling up of the numerous gaps in the printed works, and he deserves, together with his co-editors, the gratitude of every student of the subject. Dales also has the merit of having explored Grosseteste's conception of the passion of Christ and highlighted its unusual nature.[2] The further progress of that enquiry will depend, of course, upon the full edition of the writings of Grosseteste and upon continued research into his sources. Although that desideratum is still far from being fulfilled, it may be a fitting tribute to Richard Dales to extend his pursuit of this theme.

The aim of this study is to present an extract from an unedited sermon of Grosseteste which explores the nature of Christ's redemptive suffering, in line with already known writings of Grosseteste which address the same theme. The authenticity of the sermon, which is attributed to Grosseteste in the sole known manuscript witness, will be examined. Finally, a source will be put forward for each of the two parts into which Grosseteste's idea of the passion falls, namely, the soul's natural desire and care for the body, and the infinite nature of the suffering of Christ.

I

The Oxford, Bodleian Library, MS 867 contains an extensive miscellaneous collection of sermons compiled probably in the latter part of the fourteenth century or the early part of the fifteenth. Following up an attribution of one sermon in the codex to Grosseteste, noted by Tanner, S. H. Thomson recorded the rubric, *Sermo Roberti lincolniensis de triplici ierarchia humana.*[3] The sermon in question is written on folios 104r-110v in a large, round, uneven bookhand. The hand is not easy to read, and the codex has suffered some damage with the result that the folios have warped, as though the book had been dried out after having been exposed to damp. The sermon on the threefold hierarchy has the incipit, "Cum in ierarchia celesti ix distinguantur ordines scilicet 3 . . . ," and the explicit, ". . . vehemens ad suplicium peccatorum."

This sermon contains an extensive reflection on the suffering of Christ, one that matches in general outline and in a host of details the very unusual and individual ideas of Grosseteste on the death of Jesus Christ, true God and true man. The very presence of this notion is sufficient to confirm the attribution of the work to Robert Grosseteste. Even the context in which the reflection on the suffering of Christ arises can be paralleled elsewhere in his writings: all believers being one in Christ should unite their sufferings with his redemptive work, but those within the Church who undertake to live by vows are especially bound to grieve and do penance for sin, which brought about the death of the saviour; and not for their own sins merely nor for the sins of their brethren, or even of all Christians, but indeed for those of all mankind.

The relevant portion of this lengthy doctrinal sermon has been extracted from a copy of the Latin text,[4] with scriptural references added to the English translation.

> The suffering of Christ by which he satisfied for our sins with infinite pain, as Anselm proves,[5] transcends every suffering of others; therefore we are bound not only to be of one mind with Christ, according as the apostle says in our translation, "you are all one in Christ" (Gal. 3.28), but to be all of us as it were one Christ, as another translation explicitly says; in such a way that even though our grief, or the penalty for the wiping out in us of sin cannot possibly be intensified to infinity from ourselves, according to Anselm, nevertheless by the fact that we are as it were all of us one Christ, our suffering together with his suffering may be an infinite satisfaction for an infinite sin. It is clear, however, from what follows that the suffering of Christ, by which he made satisfaction for us, was infinite.
>
> Only an infinite power can possibly separate the soul or life from the body, if the latter is healthy and its natural powers have contracted no deficiency. For no finite created power, however great it might be, could possibly withdraw even the tiniest form of life from its subject, unless the natural forces and the natural heat,

by the intermediary of which life itself adheres to its subject, were debilitated; if the entire force of the world were put together it would not remove the vegetable life from a plant, unless the heat and the humour of the plant itself were in some way weakened. But the body of Christ on the cross was in its full health, and so no natural force could weaken its natural powers against his will. Only therefore the infinite virtue and the infinite power which transcends all natural virtues was able to withdraw his life from his body in the state in which it was. Now this is what he himself said in John: "I have the power to lay down my life and to take it up again" (John 10.18), and in another place, "I lay it down and no one takes it from me" (John 10.18). But the pain and grief in the very withdrawing of life is in direct proportion to the power by which life is withdrawn against the course of nature (*violenter*). Therefore, since that power was boundless, the grief was equally so [. . .].

Furthermore, what is possessed with love cannot be lost without grief. Therefore the greater the love that unites the lover with the beloved, the greater the grief experienced in the separation and the loss of the beloved. Now the soul of Christ clung with an infinite love to that most incomparable body which was united inseparably to the deity itself; it is certain that his soul loved its union with his body in proportion to the good represented by the union of his body to the deity itself, that is to say, an infinite good. Whence it follows that the love of the bond with the body was infinite, and it follows from that that the suffering in the separation of soul and body was infinite.

If therefore there has to be such grief for a single mortal sin [as Christ experienced in his crucifixion], how great should be the grief of those men living under vow who must grieve not for their own sins alone, nor solely for the sins of their brethren or for those of Christians generally, but beyond that still for the sins of all men now living, and of all future generations!

II

The argument as it is expounded by Grosseteste can without difficulty be put into quasi-formal shape:

1. Human grief and suffering cannot be infinite;
   but we are all one Christ, and the suffering of Christ was infinite;
   therefore our suffering when taken together with that of Christ is infinite.
2. Only an infinite power can separate the soul from the still-healthy body;
   but the body of Christ was still-healthy;
   therefore the power that separated the soul of Christ from his body was infinite.
3. Grief is proportionate to the power by which the soul is separated from its body;
   therefore the grief of Christ was infinite.
4. Love of union and grief at separation are proportionate;

but the union of Christ's body with God was an infinite good;
therefore the soul of Christ clung to his body with an infinite love;
therefore his grief in the separation of his soul from his body was infinite.

5. Infinite satisfaction is required for an infinite offense;
but mortal sin is an infinite offense;
therefore mortal sin requires an infinite satisfaction.
6. Those who grieve for their sins grieve for an infinite offense;
therefore their grief must be boundless.
Those who grieve for a boundless number of offenses must grieve without bound.

The reader must be struck equally by the originality of the reflections and by their logical, almost syllogistic formulation. Grosseteste retains, here as elsewhere, the style of the teacher of Aristotelian logic he once had been.

III

In his edition of Grosseteste's sermon *Ex rerum initiatarum*, Fr. Servus Gieben enumerated a series of passages containing Grosseteste's singular idea on the death of Christ.[6] These are as follows: (*a*) the sermon *Tota pulchra es*;[7] (*b*) the *Commentary on Psalms 1-100*;[8] (*c*) the *Chasteau d'Amour*;[9] (*d*) the sermon *Ex rerum initiatarum* itself;[10] and (*e*) *De cessatione legalium*.[11] To this list must now be added the *Sermo de triplici hierarchia*. Also, Grosseteste's gloss on 1 Cor. 15.55 invokes the notion of the soul's care for the body, though without applying it to the passion of Christ.[12] The intention here is to analyze this gloss and the two sermons, together with *De cessatione legalium* and the *Sermo de triplici hierarchia*, in order to determine how the idea under discussion developed at the hands of its author.

If the sermon contained in the Bodley manuscript, for which no date of composition has yet been proposed, is left until last, a look may be taken at each of the other texts in their probable order of composition, attention being paid in each case to the context in which the idea is propounded.

1. The Gloss on 1 Cor. 15.55: "Ubi est mors victoria tua?"

It is often difficult to decide where exactly a quotation from Grosseteste begins and ends within Gascoigne's dictionary articles, and normally the only indication of a contextual kind is given by the Pauline locus. The twenty line gloss addresses itself to the difference between the corruptible state of the body following the sin of Adam, and its incorruptible glorified state. It can be summarized as follows.

> The separation of the soul from the body is unavoidable, granted the continual and irreparable slide of the body towards death and corruption. The soul, however, desires to save the body; it restores it in so far as possible and it desires the lasting and continued union between the body and itself. Death triumphs over this natural desire, but victory over death comes with the soul's embrace of its body made unchangingly perfect and without any remainder of corruptibility. In that state death is absorbed into life as a privation is absorbed by a *habitus*, as emptiness by fullness, deficiency by perfection.

In this gloss the idea of the soul's profound union with the body in this life and its continued natural desire for reunion with the body in the glorified state is expressed through the notions of natural desire (*appetitus, nisus*) and of caring (*salvare, reparare*). However, there is no mention of the infinite suffering of the soul of Jesus as it was undergoing separation from his body in death.

There is good evidence that the glosses on Paul preceded the completion of the *Expositio in Epistolam ad Galatas*, which cannot unfortunately be dated with exactitude, but is certainly a mature work of Grosseteste the theologian, bearing as it does references to teaching and disputing. It was composed before 1235, and perhaps before 1230.

2. *DE CESSATIONE LEGALIUM* 3.6.8-9

The third *particula* is devoted to the divinity and the incarnation of Jesus Christ, who was the Messiah promised in the Old Testament (the theme of the second *particula*), come to liberate mankind from the fall and its penalty, through the suffering of the cross. After showing how the gospel miracles prove the divinity of Christ, Grosseteste remarks that "as it seems to me," his death on the cross was the most evident sign of all that he is divine.

Since the soul has a natural desire for its union with the body and dreads nothing so much as the separation imposed by death, it lies beyond the power of any creature to divide the soul from the body for as long as body and heart are sound; if the vital heat has not yet deserted the heart the soul cannot be separated naturally from the body. The power that separates the soul from the still-healthy body is not human but divine, the same as originally joined the soul to the organic body. So it was by his divine power that the Lord Jesus on the cross freely and of his own will breathed forth his spirit. Now clearly, at the moment of his death his vital members were still sound, for the perforation of hands and feet without any further wound would not have caused sufficient loss of blood to claim his life in only three hours of suffering; he should have retained the blood of the heart and of the interior organs, and his vital heat, for longer, as a young, strong and healthy man. That it was not loss of blood that brought about his death is evident from the fact that the opening of his side after he had expired brought forth a flow of blood; now, if a dead body is opened, even if it has not suffered prior blood loss, it will not bleed for the blood will be in a cold and coagulated state.

There is still more evidence at the passion for his divinity, Grosseteste continues, for just before he died he called forth in a loud voice, articulately and meaningfully, in prayer to God the Father, "Into your hands I commend my spirit." Now if he were merely a man, and his blood supply and vital warmth had already given out, he could not have cried aloud as he did. Therefore either he still retained the vital heat, or he was more than a mere man, or both. If he was more than a man then he was God, since there is no nature in between; if, however, his vital heat was not exhausted, then he did not die from the violence of his wounds but in virtue of that power which alone can join soul to body and alone can sunder the soul from a body still functioning naturally and with vital heat; divine power, in other words. Whence the centurion, seeing that he had died while crying aloud, acknowledged that this man was truly the Son of God. Grosseteste goes on to show the divinity of Christ from the darkening of the earth and of the sun at his death.

In the gloss on Corinthians, the first text, Grosseteste expressed the natural desire of the soul for union with the body, a desire not overcome by their separation in death. That idea in its core is now taken up in a different context, no longer that of glorification but of the redemptive suffering of Christ. Grosseteste has pondered the passion narratives with curious love: he has noted Pilate's surprise at the brevity of the passion of Jesus; meditated on the freedom of Christ's self sacrifice; imagined the loud but perfectly articulate cry of prayer (not a simple cry of suffering, he notes);[13] and placed himself in faith at the side of the centurion who, observing the strength of the voice of Christ immediately before his death, and hearing its message, acknowledged his divinity.

De cessatione legalium refers back to the *Expositio in Galatas*, which in turn came after the glosses on Paul.[14]

3. SERMON, *TOTA PULCHRA ES*

This sermon cannot be dated with certainty, but in the light of the close parallels it shows with the concept of *purgatio* as developed in Grosseteste's *Commentary on the Celestial Hierarchy* (c. 1239-41), it should be contemporary with the latter work or come after it.[15]

In the context, Grosseteste shows by the unity of the virtues[16] that the Virgin Mary excels all other human beings in prudence, fortitude, temperance and justice, and he turns to her participation in the passion of her son for proof. The sword that pierced her heart (Luke 2.35) was none other than the crucifixion: his passion was joined by her compassion. Others who have suffered realize that they are being justly punished for their sins, or that in

God's mercy, which allows them to suffer innocently, they will have all the greater reward. But Mary had no alleviation of that kind, knowing as she did the perfect innocence of her son. Now, the suffering of Christ was incomparably greater than that of any other person because it was most shameful, and it was at the same time most bitter, granted that his body was still in a healthy state, full of vital heat. The separation of the soul from the body in such circumstances is very difficult and lies beyond all human power, since no one can die while the natural heat is still strong in the heart. The separation of the soul of Jesus Christ was done against the natural desire of his soul to be united with his body; hence its extreme painfulness.

Since the Virgin Mary shared in some way in the passion and death of her son, her grief was greater than the grief of any other and her fortitude therefore beyond that of all others.[17]

4. SERMON, *EX RERUM INITIATARUM*

The idea found in *De cessatione legalium* and again in the sermon *Tota pulchra es* reappears in summary form in the long, intricate and doctrinally rich sermon on the redemption which, because of its absorption of themes from the theology of the pseudo-Dionysius, should probably be placed around the same time as Grosseteste's translation and commentary (1230-1243), or after then. Since Grosseteste teaches the doctrine of the immaculate conception in it, the sermon should be placed in time after *Tota pulchra es*, which expresses only its possibility.[18]

Grosseteste argues that the redemptive suffering of Christ was greater than any suffering ever undergone in history. Suffering is the experienced deprivation of a good desired, hence the greatest possible suffering is the most deeply felt deprivation of what is most, and most naturally, desired. Now life itself and the union of the soul with a body that is healthy and abounding in blood and natural heat is the object of the greatest and most natural of desires. That desire is so strong that no created power, however multiplied, is capable of breaking the bond uniting the soul to its healthy body, or of separating it from a heart that still has abundant blood and vital heat. So, the greatest of sufferings is the experienced deprivation of the soul in its separation from the still healthy body and heart; it transcends by far every suffering that can be inflicted by a mere creature.[19]

The theme remains the same in essence as that propounded in *De cessatione legalium* and the sermon *Tota pulchra es*, but the emphasis has changed with the new context, namely, the redemption of all mankind by the God-man, in an immolation that transcends all the suffering of history and so redeems the entire race. Christ's suffering could not have been inflicted by any creaturely power, since no created power can separate the soul from the still-healthy body.

IV

Among the texts summarized or translated the *Sermo de triplici hierarchia*, although still expressing the same idea found in the other passages and including the notion of the soul's care for the body (which is found without any association with the passion of Christ in the gloss on 1 Cor. 15.55), stands out for its originality: in it a new stress is placed upon the infinite nature of the suffering of Christ. The familiar argument is as it were generalized by means of an appeal to infinite power: no finite power could withdraw even the most insignificant form of life from its subject; Christ's soul loved its union with his body with an infinite love; if the power that effected the separation of the soul of Christ from his body was infinite, then his suffering was likewise infinite.

Note must be made, besides, of the emphasis placed upon the freedom of Christ, true God and true man, by the idea that no natural power could disjoin the soul of Christ from his body against his will.

Only in this argument does Grosseteste make an appeal to a source, one which, even if he had not led us explicitly in that direction, would have certainly been suggested by his infinity argument: St. Anselm of Canterbury.

To summarize: the *Sermo de triplici hierarchia* contains every significant element present in the other texts, when allowance is made for the specific context, which accounts for his introducing the notion by referring to the unity of Christians with Christ in his suffering.[20] The sermon contains both parts of the notion expressed in the other texts, viz. the soul's natural desire for union with the body, a desire not stilled by death; and the death which Christ freely underwent, not brought about by the wounds in his hands and feet. The argument of the sermon generalizes the key idea by an explicit appeal to the opposition of finite and infinite power. The sermon must therefore be a mature and late work of Grosseteste, contemporary with *Ex rerum initiatarum* or later than it.

V

At this point it is appropriate to take the two parts of Grosseteste's argument separately and look for a source of each. In the first place, where did Grosseteste get the idea that the soul, united as it is to the body by a powerful natural bond, cares for it and looks after it?

While Grosseteste was composing his commentary on Galatians, one of the books of reference which he had open upon his desk (alongside the Greek New Testament, the commentary of Jerome, the *Glossa ordinaria* and the gloss of Peter Lombard) was Chrysostom's *Homilies on the Epistle to Galatians*, a work upon which he drew copiously well outside of the passages he chose actually to paraphrase.[21] This source of Grosseteste has not hitherto been noticed, for the very good reason that no trace survives of any medieval Latin translation of the *Homilies*.

When St. John Chrysostom comes to Gal. 5.17 ("For the flesh lusts against the spirit and the spirit against the flesh, for these are contrary to one another"), he reacts strongly against the Manichaean interpretation of a passage which was a *locus classicus* for the sect.[22] He counters their interpretation by claiming, quite legitimately, that Paul uses "the flesh" habitually to mean not the body as such but the depraved will, so that the blame rests not upon the physical body but upon the slothful soul. Under the terms "body" and "soul" are meant two mental states, not two contrary natures; because if two natures were meant their opposition would annihilate one another, like fire and water or darkness and light. He continues:

> But if the soul cares for the body and takes great forethought on its account, and suffers a thousand things in order not to leave it, and resists its separation from it; and if the body too ministers to the soul and conveys to it much knowledge, and is adapted to its operations, how can they be contrary and conflicting with each other? For my part, I perceive by their acts that they are not only not contrary but closely accordant and attached one to another.[23]

Grosseteste's glosses, as they survive in Gascoigne's quotations, do not yield certain evidence of his study of Greek; his *Expositio in Epistolam ad Galatas*, on the other hand, the sole Pauline work of his to survive in finished form, certainly does so. His gloss on 1 Cor. 15.55 shows no evidence that he has read Chrysostom, but the remainder of the texts examined suggests that he had. Against the Manichaeans, Chrysostom asserts that soul and body are not contrary to each other but adapted to each other as complementary parts of a unity; hence the soul cares for the body and provides for it, and the body ministers to the soul, acquiring sense-knowledge for it. Chrysostom may have been influenced by the Stoic motif of *oikeiosis*, for self preservation and the continuance of life in the body appear as the soul's resistance to leaving it. The necessary corollary of natural union is explicit in the passage quoted, viz. the resistance of the soul to separation from the body, and its suffering in leaving it.

This leads to a hypothesis, namely that Grosseteste read this notion in conjunction with a similar but unrelated argument of Anselm, and that it was that conjunction which gave him his particular idea of the infinite suffering of Christ on the cross.

Why did Grosseteste not quote Chrysostom in any of the texts which have been examined here? It can only be suggested, in answer to this question, that the homilies of Chrysostom on Galatians were not available to Latin readers (except to Grosseteste himself) to take up the reference. In his own exposition of Gal. 5.17 he chose to pursue a related line of thought, found in an anti-Manichaean argument in book one of Augustine's *De doctrina Christiana*, a reference which he presumably considered more useful to his readers, and accessible besides. It is the writer's belief that Grosseteste none the less did reflect upon the idea of Chrysostom, but that only its conjunction with his reading of the *Cur Deus homo* of Anselm gave him the full idea in its two constituent parts.

VI

Anselm remained rather neglected in the twelfth century, but the rediscovery of his genius was under way in the first half of the thirteenth, and Grosseteste was in the lead in that movement.[24] His influence upon Grosseteste's argument about the death of Christ is only one of a number of influences (certainly not all traced as yet) upon the writings of the bishop of Lincoln.

For the author of *Cur Deus homo*, Christ willed to die rather than leave the world without salvation, but he died "nulla necessitate sed libera voluntate":

> Et ipse dicit: "Ego pono animam meam, ut iterum sumam eam. Nemo tollit eam a me, sed ego pono eam a me ipso. Potestatem habeo ponendi eam et potestatem habeo iterum sumendi eam."[25]

Now here is the same text from John 10.17-18 which Grosseteste was to employ in his *Sermo de triplici hierarchia*.

Was Christ free in offering his life? Anselm pursues his argument in *Cur Deus homo* 2.11: Christ is free to lay down his life and to take it up again, otherwise he is not all-powerful. Since death followed sin into the world, but Christ is sinless, he did not have to die or be put to death. Yet the nature of sin required satisfaction in suffering:

> **Anselm**: If man sinned through enjoyment, is it not fitting that he should make satisfaction through bitter suffering [*per asperitatem*]? And if he was vanquished by the devil to God's dishonor, in sinning so easily that nothing easier could there be, is it not just that the man who will satisfy for sin should overcome the devil for the honor of God, with a difficulty of such proportion that there could be none greater? Is it not right that, to the extent that he removed himself from God by sinning, in such a way that he could not remove himself further, he should give himself to God in making satisfaction, in such a way that he could not give himself more?
>
> **Boso:** Nothing is more reasonable.
>
> **Anselm**: Well, there is nothing more bitter or more difficult that man can suffer for the honor of God, of his own free will and not as something owed, than death, and in no way other than in death can a man give himself more to God for his honor.
>
> **Boso**: All that is true.

Anselm: He who would wish to satisfy for the sin of man must be capable of dying, if he wishes to.

Boso: I can see clearly that the man we are looking for must be someone who neither dies of necessity, since he is all-powerful, nor dies for a debt due, since he will never be a sinner; someone who will be able to die by his own free will, for that will be necessary.[26]

Asperitas and *difficultas* are terms which Grosseteste repeated in his argument, thinking of this passage of Anselm. The infinity theme, so typical of Anselm's thought, is echoed in Grosseteste's argument concerning the passion of Christ. And the freedom of Christ, which is the whole context of the argument of Anselm, is reflected in Grosseteste's idea that Christ's body was not overcome in its natural resources of blood and heat, but that his life (i.e., the union of his soul with his body) was voluntarily sundered by his divine will, with a suffering and difficulty greater than which cannot be, or be conceived.

VII

Grosseteste's idea, which resulted from the meeting in his mind of a suggestion of Chrysostom with an argument of Anselm, retains a certain originality. It has not as such been traced to any known source, nor does it appear to have had much by way of posterity. It may well be asked why such a striking idea did not achieve significance in the schools. It cannot be that theological readers confused it with the heresy of docetism and hence gave it a wide berth, for Grosseteste insists to infinity on the reality of the body of Christ, and on its union with his soul and with his divine personhood. If the idea he thought out so clearly, and to which, quite evidently, he was resolutely attached, failed to gain attention, then that was doubtless because there simply is something implausible about it. Grosseteste made no allowance for the weakened state of Christ as he approached his crucifixion, debilitated by an entire night of agony and torture; and he gives no sign of realizing that the death of the crucified resulted not so much from the loss of blood as from asphyxiation, which came about when the sufferer nailed to his cross became gradually, but ever so painfully, incapable of supporting by the waning strength of his transfixed wrists and feet the ever-increasing weight of his tortured body.

Notes

[1] Servus Gieben, O.F.M. Cap., has noted the presence of the idea in the *Moralitates in Evangelia* (Oxford, Trinity College, MS c. 50, fol. 234rb); see his article "Robert Grosseteste on Preaching, with the Edition of the Sermon *Ex rerum initiatarum* on Redemption," *Collectanea Franciscana* 37

(1967). If this work is no longer to be attributed to Grosseteste, then it contains the only independent invocation of Grosseteste's idea yet discovered. E. J. Dobson impressively attacks both the external and the internal evidence purporting to authenticate the *Moralia* as a work of Grosseteste, in *Moralities on the Gospels: A New Source of "Ancrene Wisse"* (Oxford, 1975). Sir Richard Southern thinks there is no solid support for the attribution of the work to Grosseteste; see his *Robert Grosseteste: The Growth of an English Mind in the Middle Ages* (Oxford, 1986), p. 31 n. 8.

[2] Richard C. Dales, "Robert Grosseteste on the Soul's Care for the Body," to be printed among the papers delivered at the Grosseteste Colloquium, held at the Warburg Institute, London, on May 29 and 30, 1987. The papers will appear as a volume of the Warburg series. Dales's article includes the text of Grosseteste's gloss on 1 Cor 15.55, which will be considered below.

[3] S. Harrison Thomson, *The Writings of Robert Grosseteste, Bishop of Lincoln 1235-1253* (Cambridge, 1940), p. 181.

[4] See Appendix 1 for the edited Latin text. Wyclyf incorporated an extract from this sermon of "Lincolniensis" into his *De civili dominio*, but did not include the portion printed here. His is the only use of the sermon known to me. See *De civili dominio* 3:85-87, ed. Johann Loserth (London, Wyclif Society, 1903), and my Appendix 3.

[5] In *Cur Deus homo*. This source will be discussed near the conclusion of this paper.

[6] Gieben, "Grosseteste on Preaching," p. 132 n. 209.

[7] Servus Gieben, O.F.M. Cap., "Robert Grosseteste on the Immaculate Conception, with the Text of the Sermon *Tota pulchra es*," *Collectanea Franciscana* 28 (1958), 226.

[8] Bologna, Archiginnasio, MS A. 983, fol. 88ra. I have not had access to this work.

[9] Ed. J. Murray (Paris, 1918), lines 1145-80, p. 121.

[10] Gieben, "Grosseteste on Preaching," p. 132 n. 209..

[11] *Robert Grosseteste: De cessatione legalium* 3.6.6-9, ed. Richard C. Dales and Edward B. King, Auctores Britannici Medii Aevi 6 (London, 1986), pp. 150-51. To this list Gieben added the work *Moralitates in Evangelia*; see n. 1.

[12] Edited by Richard Dales among the glosses of Grosseteste on the Epistles of St. Paul preserved by Thomas Gascoigne in his *De veritate* (Oxford, Lincoln College, MSS lat. 117 [I] and 118 [II]). These glosses will be published in the British Academy series along with the present writer's edition of Grosseteste's *Expositio in Epistolam ad Galatas*. I am grateful to Richard Dales for the extended loan, in 1985, of his photomechanical copy of *De veritate*.

[13] "Praeterea, voce magna clamans expiravit, nec clamans clamore gemitus sed clamosa prolacione vocis litterate et significative et Patrem Deum suppliciter deprecantis, dicens: *In manus tuas commendo spiritum meum*. Si autem purus homo fuisset et defecissent in interioribus sanguis et calor vitalis, nullo modo clamare sic potuisset . . . Unde et centurio, videns quia sic clamans expirasset ait, *Vere hic homo Filius Dei erat*." *De cessatione legalium* 3.6.9 (p. 151).

[14] Ibid., 1.11.1 (p. 68) and 4.6.8 (p. 179).

[15] James McEvoy, *The Philosophy of Robert Grosseteste* (Oxford, 1982 [corr. reprint 1986]), p. 498.

[16] A Stoic theme which Grosseteste found in Seneca.

[17] "Christi quoque passio incomparabiliter fuit maior cuiusque alterius passione, non solum quia eius mors fuit probrosissima, sed, ut puto, quia fuit etiam acerbissima. Deposuit enim animam suam in corpore suo sano, habente adhuc caloris vitalis plenitudinem. Sed segregatio animae a corpore sano, in quo viget calor naturalis, difficillima est, quia etiam supra omnem humanam potentiam est. Nullus enim moritur vel mori potest dum viget calor naturalis in corde. Illa igitur segregatio animae Jesu Christi a corpore suo sano difficillima fuit, maximeque contraria naturali appetitui animae, quae naturaliter appetit coniungi cum corpore. Ideoque fuit acerbitatis maximae. Cum igitur beata Virgo hanc quodammodo compatiendo sustinuit passionem et mortem, ipsius dolor aliorum exsuperavit dolores et ideo eius fortitudo aliorum fortitudines." *Tota pulchra es*, ed. Gieben, pp. 226-27.

[18] McEvoy, *The Philosophy of Robert Grosseteste*, pp. 498-99.

[19] "Cum autem poena sit sensata privatio boni appetiti, maxime poena est maxime sensata privatio maxime et naturalissime appetiti. Maxime autem, et appetitu maxime naturaliter appetitur haec vita et unio animae cum corpore sano et corde abundante sanguine et calore vitali. Et iste est appetitus tam fortis, quod nulla vis creata, quantumcumque immultiplicata, non [*understand* nec] posset rumpere vinculum unionis animae cum corpore sano, nec eam separare a corde, sanguine et calore vitali adhuc abundante. Summa igitur poenarum est sensata privatio et separatio animae a corpore et corde adhuc sano, et superexcellens omnem poenam a pura creatura inferri possibilem. Hanc igitur poenam oportet offerre voluntarie Deum-hominem Patri, et sibi Deo, et Spiritui Sancto, uni et indiviso rei publicae universitatis gubernatori in reconciliationem generis humani, potentia et virtute suae divinitatis, in infinitum excedente omnem virtutem et potentiam creatam, faciente hanc suae animae a corpore et corde suo adhuc sano separationem." *Ex rerum initiatarum*, ed. Gieben, p. 132.

[20] Concerning the unity of all the redeemed in Christ the sermon refers to "another translation" in the following terms: "Debemus nos non solum esse unum animi christo secundum quod dicit apostolus in nostra translacione, *omnes vos unum estis in christo*, sed etiam omnes quasi unus Christus, prout expresse dicit alia translacio, ita scilicet quod quamvis dolor noster vel vindictum pro peccato absolvendo in nobis etiam ex nobis non possit in infinitum intendi secundum illud anselmi, in eo tamen quod quasi omnes unus christus sumus nostra pena una cum pena eius possit esse satisfactio infinita pro peccato infinito."

In several places Grosseteste reflects upon the nature of this union, which has a number of dimensions and which transcends unity of will in the direction of something more profound still, namely, the unity of our nature in the Incarnate Word. On two occasions he refers to the Greek of St. Paul at Gal. 3.28, where εἷς (*unus*) has become *unum* in the Vulgate. That he attached a good deal of importance to this difference is evident both from the sermon itself and from the two following passages, the first of which comes from *De cessatione legalium* 3.1.16 (p. 125): "Nunc autem sumus filii adopcionis per hoc quod sumus *unum in Christo*, ut dicit apostolus, sive ut habetur in littera greca *unus in Christo*, qui est filius naturalis. Sed hanc unitatem qua sumus unum vel unus in Christo non facit solum conformitas voluntatis nostre cum voluntate christi, sed cum hoc etiam unitas nature in qua communicamus cum Christo."

The second passage comes from his unprinted comment on Gal. 3.28 (Oxford, Magdalen College, MS lat. 57, fol. 14r): "Et possunt in his tribus condivisionibus intelligi genera omnium proprietatum, quibus homines apud homines gloriosi aut ignominiosi sunt. Et quia haec sunt aut proprietates quae sunt in corpore, quae dantur intelligi per *masculum et feminam*; aut relationes actuales ad exteriora quae dantur intelligi per *liberum et servum*; aut relationes naturales ad exteriora quae dantur intelligi per *Iudaeum et Graecum*, haec enim significant relationem naturalem ad gentes et ad patriam; et vere haec non faciunt distinctionem in praedicta filiatione, quia quotquot per huiusmodi proprietates sunt distincti, *in Christo sunt unum* et unus Christus. In graeco autem habetur *unus estis in Christo*; et quis unus nisi Christus? Sicut enim ait Gregorius crebro in *Moralibus*, Christus et ecclesia, caput et corpus, sunt una persona, unus scilicet Christus. *Nemo* enim *ascendit in caelum, nisi qui descendit de caelo*, unus videlicet Christus. Sicut e contra, ut idem Gregorius ait, diabolus cum corpore suo sunt una persona. Quomodo enim non esset ecclesia cum Christo una persona, quemadmodum corpus cum anima est una persona, cum ipse Christus sit vita ecclesiae vivificans, continens, movens et regens eam sicut anima corpus, et singulos qui sunt de ecclesia sicut anima singula corporis membra. Aut quemadmodum dicere potest corpus et singulum corporis membrum, cum iam animatur postquam fuit non animatum: 'Vivo ego, iam non ego, vivit vero in me anima,' sic dicere potest ecclesia et singulum ecclesiae membrum: *Vivo ego, iam non ego, vivit vero in me Christus*. Huic consonat Augustinus in X. libro *De trinitate*, exponens hoc verbum quod est in Iohanne: *ut sint unus, sicut et nos unum sumus*, ita inquiens: 'Non dixit, Sicut ego et ipsi unum sumus, quamvis per id, quod *ecclesiae caput est*, et *corpus eius* ecclesia posset dicere: Sicut ego et ipsi [non] unum sed unus sumus, quia caput et corpus unus est Christus.' Nec solum sumus omnes unus in Christo, sed et sumus unum in illo. Et forte est inter haec aliqua differentia: unus enim sumus in Christo quia, ut dictum est, una persona quae est

Christus: unum vero, quia cum simus omnes unius naturae habemus insuper in ipso et per ipsum *cor unum et animam unam*, et participes facti sumus illius naturae per gratiam, cuius ille aeternaliter est particeps per naturam. Propter participationem ergo unius naturae cum Christo, id est, divinae naturae, dicimur omnes unum in illo."

[21] The Greek text of the *Homilies on the Epistle to Galatians* of St. John Chrysostom was first edited by H. Savile (Eton: 1612-13); this edition was copied by Migne, PG 61:611-82, who accompanied it with a Latin translation of the sixteenth century, the earliest Latin version of the work.

[22] I have prepared a study of Grosseteste's utilization of the *Homilies* of Chrysostom as revealed in his commentary on Galatians. It should be published before very long. It seems altogether likely that Grosseteste was directly following the Greek text.

[23] Quoted from the anonymous English translation in *A Library of Fathers of the Holy Catholic Church* (Oxford, 1849), 5:84.

[24] Michael Robson, O.F.M. Conv., delivered a paper to the Grosseteste Colloquium on "St. Anselm, Robert Grosseteste and the Franciscan Tradition." It will appear with the collected papers (see n. 2).

[25] *Cur Deus homo* 1.10.

[26] Ibid., 2.11 (my version).

Appendix 1

The following is the relevant portion of the Latin text from Robert Grosseteste's *Sermo de triplici hierarchia*, transcribed from the Oxford, Bodleian Library, MS 867, folios 104v-105r.[1] Abbreviations of one or two letters (e.g., the name of Christ) have been silently expanded, but most have been completed within square brackets. Proposed corrections are clearly marked off by square brackets within the text. At one point it has not been possible to make any sense of what is written (i.e., at the words, "et huius mur di ce tantum quos omnes qui tantum"); this phrase is therefore omitted from the literal translation, but its absence has been clearly marked.

> Cum pena christi qua satisfecit pro peccatis nostris infinita acerbitate ut probat ansel[mus] excedat omnem penam aliorum, debemus nos non solum esse unum animi christo secundum quod dicit apos[tolus] in nostra transalacione [*sic*], omnes vos unum estis in christo, sed etiam omnes quasi unus christus, prout expresse dicit alia translacio, ita scil[icet] quod qua vis [*sic*; *read* quamvis] dolor noster vel mundcam [*sic*; *read* vindictum] pro peccato absolute [*sic*; *read* absolvendo] in nobis etiam ex nobis non possit in infinitum intendi scil angeli [*sic*; *read* secundum illud anselmi], in eo tamen quod quasi omnes [105r] unus christus sumus nostra pena una cum pena eius possit esse satisfactio infinita pro peccato infinito. Quod autem pena christi quasi [*sic*; *read* qua] satisfecit pro nobis fuerit infinita sic patet. in possibilem [*sic*; *read* impossibile] animam sine [*sic*; *read* sive] vitam separari a corpore sano cuius vires naturales nullum summunt defectum, nisi per infinitam

potenciam. omnis enim finita potencia et creata quantumcumque fuerit magna nonposset abstrahere minimam vitam a suo subiecto nisi debilitatis viribus naturalibus et calore naturali quibus mediantibus adherat [*sic*; *read* adheret] ipsa vita suo subiecto. tota enim virtus mundana simul unita non auferret plante suam vitam vegetabilem nisi debilitato aliquo modo calore et humore ipsius plante. set corpus christi in cruce fuit in plena sanitate, cuius vires naturales [n]ulla vis naturalis ipso invito posset debilitare. ergo suam vitam a tali corpore abstrahere non potuit nisi virtus infinita et potencia infinita que est super omnes virtutes naturales. et hoc est quod ipse dixit in io[hanne]: potestatem habeo ponendi animam meam et iterum su[mendi]. et alibi, ego pono eam et nemo eam tollit a me. sed quanta est potencia quanta [*sic*; *read* qua] vita violenter abstrahitur, tanto maior est pena et dolor in ipsa abstraccione. ergo cum infinita fuit potencia et infinitus fuit dolor, et huius mur di ce tantum quos omnes qui tantum. item non sum [*sic*; *read* sine] dolore amittitur quod cum amore possidetur. ergo quanto maior est [amor *added above line*] uniens amantem cum amato, tanto maior sencietur dolor in dissolucione et amissione amati. sed infinito amore adherebat anima christi tam excellentissimo corpori quod inseparabiliter fuit unitum ipsi deitati, constat enim quod tantum amavit uniri cum corpore quantum bonum fuit ipsius corporis[2] unio ad ipsam deitatem, et hoc fuit bonum infinitum. ergo infinitus fuit amor ipsius inherencie. ergo infinitus fuit dolor in separacione, si ergo tantus debet esse dolor premio [*sic*; *read* pro uno] mortali peccato, quantus debet esse dolor ipsorum virorum religiosorum qui non solum debent dolore [*sic*; *read* dolere] pro suis peccatis, nec solum pro peccatis fratrum, nec solum pro peccatis christianorum, immo etiam pro peccatis omnium hominum, et non solum precencium [*sic*; *read* presencium] set futurorum.

Notes

[1] I am grateful to my former colleague at Queen's University, Belfast, Pamela Robinson (now at the Institute of Romance Studies of the University of London), for her careful checking of my transcription, but assume full responsibility for it. I am not aware of the existence of any other copy.

[2] In the margin there is an addition made in the hand of the copyist: "subsequentibus scd quod frequenter promicit [*read* promisit] do^{us} filius [*read* filiis] isrl [=Israel] subvenire."

Appendix 2

Le Chasteau d'Amour is the title commonly given to the long poem written by Grosseteste on the history of salvation.[1] This is the longest poetic work in the Anglo-Norman dialect. It reflects Grosseteste's concern for the deepening of the Christian faith and life of the people. In it he conveys a rich theological content in easily memorisable verse form. The poem begins with the creation and the fall, and relates the Old Testament prophecies of the Messiah to the incarnation, redemptive death and resurrection of Christ. The allegory of a castle is intricately developed before being explained: it represents the body of the Virgin Mary in which the new king is conceived, safe from the assaults of the devil, defended by the towers of the four cardinal virtues, the courts of the virginity, chastity and marriage of Mary, the barbicans of the seven virtues and the deep moats of the spiritual poverty of Mary. The poem was translated several times into Middle English.[2]

As Servus Gieben noted, the poem contains a reference to Grosseteste's own ideas of the soul's relationship to the body, and the infinite suffering of the redeemer.[3] The passage is reproduced without change from the edition of Murray, lines 1145-84 (pp. 121-22):

Mes kant a mort se livera
Mort par sa mort rechata,
Kar plus suffri cent itant
Peines e maus en moriant,
Ke les diables n'eurent poër
A nature humaine charger.
Kar tant eime l'alme le cors
Ke jamès ne en istra fors,
Pur nule peine endurer,
Si l'em le vousist detrencher,
Einz ke le cors eit perdu,
De tuz cinc sens la vertu.
C'est le oïr e le veër,
Li odorer e le parler,
E le taster tut perdera,
Ainz ke de le cors passera,
Kar Nature ne puet suffrir
L'alme de le cors einz partir.
Mes cil ki tut poer ad
Cent feiz ses peines dublad,
Kar kant en la croiz pendi,
A haute voiz l'alme rendi.
ors mustra ke il Deus esteit.
Nostre rançon adonk feseit.
Vivant le cors, fist ço sanz faille,
E ensi venqui la bataille.
Tant ne puet le diable charger
Ne nature tant endurer.
Ha! tres gloriuse Reine
Marie, Mere e Virgine,
Pur Pité ne puis nomer
Tes dolurs ne rementiver.
Meis lores est tut acomplie
De Simeon la prophetie,
Kar plus ke al cors fu naffree
Par mi l'alme de une espee.

Mes cent feiz ta joie dubla
Kant il de mort resuscita.
Riens n'eüst valu la passion
Ne fust la resurrection.

No modern translation of the poem exists. However, a colleague at the Université Catholique de Louvain, M. Michel Francard of the *Faculté de Philosophie et Lettres*, who is a specialist in medieval French language and literature, has kindly acceded to my request for a version of the lines quoted; sincere gratitude to him for permission to print his translation is expressed herewith. In a letter to me he remarks, "S'il fallait qualifier mon travail, je parlerais de 'traduction littérale': en effet, après plusieurs essais infructueux, j'ai abandonné l'idée d'une traduction 'littéraire,' celle-ci obscurcissant trop le rapport avec le texte de base." His decision is justified by the result.

Mais quand il se livra à la mort
Il racheta la mort par sa mort,
Car si nombreux furent les peines et les maux
Qu'il souffrit en mourant
Que les diables n'eurent pas le pouvoir
De charger la nature humaine.
Car l'âme aime tant le corps
Que jamais elle ne le quittera,
Pour n'endurer aucune peine,
Si l'homme veut le (=le corps) tailler en pièces,
Plutôt que de perdre son corps,
[Ce sera] l'usage des cinq sens [qu'il perdra].
C'est l'ouíe et la vue,
L'odorat et la parole,
Et le toucher [qu'il] perdra totalement,
Mais non le corps,
Car la Nature ne peut souffrir
Que l'âme se sépare du corps.
Mais celui qui a tout pouvoir
A doublé cent fois ses peines
Car quand on le suspendit à la croix,
A haute voix il rendit l'âme.
Alors il prouva qu'il était Dieu.
Il payait alors notre rançon.
Le corps vivant, il fit cela sans faiblir,
Et ainsi il remporta la bataille.
Le diable ne peut en supporter autant
Ni la nature en endurer autant.
Ha! très glorieuse Reine
Marie, Mère et Vierge,
La Piété m'empêche d'énumérer
Tes douleurs ou de les remémorer.
Mais maintenant est totalement accomplie

La prophétie de Siméon,
Car plus qu'en ton corps, tu fus blessée
En ton âme par une épée.
Mais ta joie doubla cent fois
Quand il ressuscita de la mort.
La passion n'aurait eu aucune valeur
S'il n'y avait eu la résurrection.

The references of Grosseteste to the loud cry with which Christ died and the proof of his divinity he gave on the cross make one think at once of the *De cessatione legalium.*

Notes

[1] *Le Chasteau d'Amour*, ed. J. Murray, Paris, 1918.

[2] K. Sajavaara, ed., *The Middle English Translations of Robert Grosseteste's "Château d'Amour,"* Helsinki, 1967. The author of this work intends to prepare a critical edition of the poem.

[3] See article, n. 1.

Appendix 3

It has been noted above (n. 4 of the main text) that Wyclyf included in his *De civili dominio* 1.111 a long quotation from the sermon *De triplici hierarchia*. Since the Wyclyf edition is not always easy to lay one's hands upon and the sermon is of course unedited, it may be deemed useful to reproduce the quotation in full as it appears in Loserth's edition, with the result that the greater part of this isolated and almost unknown sermon of Grosseteste can be made available and the attention of a future editor of the sermons may be drawn to the codex 1341 of the Vienna Nationalbibliothek upon which the Loserth edition is based.

Wyclyf is arguing that professed religious cannot be dispensed from the evangelical poverty to which they are committed by their vow, and that perfect poverty, if it is to conform to the gospel and to the highest and noblest ideal of the monastic tradition, must include within the abdication of all ownership the renunciation of civil lordship. The rule of Christ is more perfect than the practices and laws that have been added on to it. He quotes from the *Rule* of St. Benedict, chap. 45, in support of his contention, and then adduces Grosseteste, likewise in support:

Cum in ierarchia celesti novem distinguantur ordines: Ad religiosos, pertinet status mundo abrenunciancium qui tripliciter distinguitur. Cum ergo tria bona sunt bona mundana corporalia et spiritualia, hiis tribus bonis debet vir religiosus abrenunciare; ita scilicet quod nec retineat sibi tale dominium nec potestatem habendi dominium. Hec est enim differencia inter secularem et religiosum quod secularis multorum bonorum exteriorum potest non habere dominium, habet tamen potestatem habendi dominium, sicut puer qui non habet equum habet tamen potestatem habendi equum, sed vir religiosus ita renunciavit omnibus quod nec dominium alicuius rei sibi retinuit nec potestatem habendi vel recuperandi dominium. Unde patere potest quod infinitum plus peccat religiosus alicuius rei proprietarius quam eciam fur secularis. Quanto est enim distancia inter non posse habere [*add* et inter non habere] tanta est distancia inter peccatum religiosi et peccatum secularis; sed constat quod infinita est distancia hinc inde. Si igitur secularis furetur equum alicuius, contrectat rem alienam invito domino, cuius scilicet non habet dominium, cum tamen potest habere, verus dominus potest illi vel dare vel vendere. Sed si vir religiosus [*Cod.*: religiosus omnium] habet proprietatem eciam unius alicuius [*Cod.*: ac'], contrectat rem alienam et furtum committit, et tanto magis furtum, quanto magis est peccatum contrectare aliquid quod nec est suum nec potest esse suum. Appetere autem quod nec est suum nec potest esse suum, est quasi elevare se in infinitum supra se; ergo cum solus Deus excedit in omnem racionalem creaturam, talem appetere eque [*add*: est] appetere se esse Deum, hoc autem appetere est velle Deum non esse, cum deitas soli conveniat. Patet ergo quantum est peccatum religiosorum proprietariorum, quibus non habere proprium nec posse habere convenit.

Unde quia supra homines se extollunt, non merentur cum hominibus sepeliri, sicut de Lucifero appetente equalitatem Dei, Ysai. XIV, capitulo XIX, XX Cod.: capitulo 9]: Cadaver putridum non habebit consorcium neque cum eis in sepultura. Hinc iustissime precepit Gregorius proprietarium extra consorcium fratrum in sterquilinium in profunda fovea proici, et tali dicendum est illud, proiecta peccunia super cadaver eius, pecunia tua tecum sit in perdicione. Nec erit hoc obprobrium religioni sed pocius in honorem et famam, cum pervenerit ad aures secularium observancia tanti rigoris; sic et primus ordo sive primus gradus mundo renunciancium est ex toto predicta exteriora bona relinquere; secundus autem est eciam bona corporalia totaliter pro aliena voluntate postponere; et non dico ad presens bona corporis qualia sunt sanitas, fortitudo et huiusmodi, sed bona corporis voco [*sic*; *read* noto (*?*)] unumquodque membrum operativum sive organicum cum actu sibi appropriato; verbi gracia oportet virum religiosum renunciare visui et organo, videndo eciam cum ipso actu videnti ut nec oculum nec actum videndi convertat ad aliquid in mundo secundum propriam voluntatem vel contra institucionem regule sue et regularis observancie quam professus est vel contra voluntatem sui superioris, similiter nec aurem nec auditum vel ipsum actum audiendi, gressum vel actum gradiendi et sic de ceteris membris comparativis cum actibus suis.

Nec minus peccat qui aliquam sibi proprietatem retinet de bono corporis, ut dictum est, quam ille qui sibi retinet aliquid proprium de bono exteriori de cuius peccati quantitate prius dictum est.

Tercius autem gradus ad idem est quod religiosus abrenunciat eciam bonis ipsius anime et specialiter proprie cognicioni vel affeccioni que vocat Bernhardus alio nomine propriam voluntatem. Nec mirum quod faciat servus cum fecit dominus qui non venit suam facere voluntatem sed voluntatem patris, ymmo sua relinquit pro voluntate patris ubi dixit: Verumtamen, non sicut ego volo sed sicut tu vis; proprium eciam sensum relinquere debet, ut non innitatur prudencie sue nec sapiens aput semet ipsum sed magis regatur sensu alieno, ymmo eciam nec meditari vel studium apponere nec affecionem suam alicui rei applicare debet secundum suam propriam ordinacionem. In hiis tribus gradibus consistit secunda ierarchia humana.

The Riddle of the Disappearing Reformer: Grosseteste by the Sixteenth Century

Elwood E. Mather, III

In recent years there has been a renewed interest in the life of Robert Grosseteste (c. 1170-1253). Controversial and often misunderstood in his own day, Grosseteste, among other things, is said to have been the first chancellor of Oxford University, a promoter of the new scientific learning, a friend to the Franciscans, and bishop of Lincoln from 1235 to 1253. Most recently, James McEvoy and Sir Richard Southern have produced fine assessments of the scholar and his work, the former in *The Philosophy of Robert Grosseteste*, and the latter in *Robert Grosseteste: The Growth of an English Mind in Medieval Europe*. Among other things, Southern covered considerable new ground with respect to an attempt at establishing a plausible chronology for the life of the Lincoln bishop and has provided what will be the new standard for excellence in this kind of study. In the work he raises a number of issues with regard to Grosseteste's influence, reputation, and impact on later philosophical, theological and reform-minded individuals in the centuries following. One of the more provocative is the assessment of Grosseteste's place in history.

S. Harrison Thomson, another pioneer in modern Grosseteste studies, saw the ghost of Grosseteste in the writings of Wyclyf, Hus and even Luther. But as far as the prophet's being accepted in his own country -- Southern believes that the great bishop did not fare as well. He seems to suggest that by the time sixteenth century Englishmen have had a glimpse of Grosseteste at the hands of John Foxe and Raphael Holinshed, either he has been metamorphosed into a proto-puritan anti-papist, unwittingly clinging to his mitre in the windstorm of late medieval change, or perhaps some sort of cruel, heartless, and even strange ecclesiastical potentate, operating with cold logic and using the bishop's crozier as a symbolic weapon with which to pummel opponents.

As Southern sees it:

> Holinshed ignored the anti-papal bishop, but extracted from Matthew Paris a portrait of a sour martinet. He chose details which portrayed a busybody bishop, who excommunicated sinners and negligent officials with a hasty hand; a prurient investigator of monastic sins, who in his visitation of monasteries 'entered into the chambers of the monks and searched their beds, and, coming to the houses of the nuns, went so near as to cause their breasts to be tried in order that he might understand their chaste livings,' and so on. All these details are indeed to be found in Matthew Paris, and it is by no means clear that Grosseteste was incapable of

> these actions. But they had lost their interest, and Grosseteste was effectively dismissed from the pages of national, still more international history for three hundred years.[1]

Southern's argument, then, is a two-fold one: that Holinshed is the culprit largely responsible for the demise of Grosseteste's reputation, and that because of this bad press the bishop of Lincoln virtually disappeared from the pages of history for three hundred years.

But is this thesis sustainable? First of all, does Grosseteste in fact vanish in the three hundred years following the publication of Holinshed's *Chronicles*? Clearly that question is problematic. What does seem to be true is that there were a number of factors in England in the sixteenth century which would seem to have led people to ask Grosseteste different questions than their ancestors might have. James McConica, in *English Humanists and Reformation Politics*, for example, suggests that already by the beginning of the sixteenth century humanistic (particularly Erasmian) teaching was beginning to gain in popularity at the expense of traditional scholastic studies.[2] If this is so, it would be a factor almost certainly suggesting a loss of academic interest in at least part of the corpus of Grosseteste literature. But more to the point regarding the bishop of Lincoln's alleged prolonged absence from the pages of history is good evidence that he did not fully disappear. J. H. Srawley notes that the bishop's tomb was destroyed by parliamentary troops in 1644, but that a drawing of the monument "appears in Dugdale's collections made in 1641 before the Civil War."[3] There are instances in the seventeenth, eighteenth and nineteenth centuries when Grosseteste's works and life were not only studied but published. The recent edition of *De cessatione legalium* cites the example of a manuscript in the Bodleian Library annotated in a seventeenth-century hand, as well as a 1658 published edition of the work.[4] Indeed, the bishop's burial chamber was even opened in 1782 when, in addition to Grosseteste's skeleton, it was found to contain "a paten and chalice, his episcopal ring, and a metal ring linking the staff to the head of the crozier."[5] One would hope this exhumation was motivated by more than simple morbid curiosity. In fact, the procedure seems to have been occasioned by the fact that the cathedral floor was to have been repaved and the tomb was "much ruinated" (still presumably from the time of the Civil War) and was in the way. It was opened in front of a few witnesses: the precentor, the organist and "one or two more members of the church,"[6] admittedly, a rather modest if not unceremonious treatment. However, the tomb was reopened about a month later by the president of the Royal Society, Sir Joseph Banks, who used his personal friendship with the precentor of the cathedral, a Rev. Dr. Gordon, to allow a second exhumation, at which time Banks had detailed sketches made of the tomb and its contents. Banks' own description of the episode is important, for it demonstrates clearly that at least in the minds of some, the reputation of Grosseteste was not unremembered:

> I felt some disappointment at having missed a sight so extraordinary; the bishop, who, in his lifetime was eminent for learning and piety, highly respected by the Clergy of his times, and at his death enjoyed the Chancelership of the University of Oxford as well as the Bishoprick of Lincoln, was likely to have been interred with all the expense and magnificence of the age he lived in, and he had been buried about 500 years; so that the remains, if any there were, of customs so antient, and the preservation in which those remains might appear after such a lapse of time, promised much to antiquarian curiosity.[7]

Later biographies of Grosseteste include the well-known work by Samuel Pegge: *Robert Grosseteste, Bishop of Lincoln*, done in 1793, and a work noted by Southern, F. S. Stevenson: *Robert Grosseteste*, published in 1899.[8] On balance, however, it is in terms of the manuscript traditions of the venerable bishop that Professor Southern's assertion is largely true. S. Harrison Thomson's *The Writings of Robert Grosseteste* does seem to reveal a significant paucity of manuscripts or editions extant from the seventeenth, eighteenth and nineteeth centuries, but the same has to be said, however, of the sixteenth century, where the manuscript transmission is already relatively limited.[9] It seems fairly clear that the levelling-off of interest in Grosseteste in academic circles, if not in popular thought, occurs well before the end of sixteenth century.

What can be said of the first part of Southern's thesis concerning Grosseteste's treatment by Holinshed? It is important to examine the information in context. It might be argued that even the first entry concerning Grosseteste, that of 1235, is cast in almost biblical language:

> About the same time, to wit the seauenth of Februarie died Hugh de Wels bishop of Lincolne, a great enimie to moonks and religious men. Robert Grosted was then preferred to his roome, a man of great learning, trained vp in schooles euen from his infancie.[10]

It also must be admitted that the bishop did excommunicate a priest and the sheriff of Rutland, but here again Holinshed's sympathies clearly lie with Lincoln. The priest was accused of incontinency, but it was because he, according to Holinshed, "continued fortie days without seeking to be reconciled," and when Grosseteste requested that the sheriff apprehend the man, as the *Chronicles* puts it, "the shiriffe winked at the matter." Though the bishop then excommunicated the sheriff, the officer escaped punishment because he was under royal jurisdiction (and protection) as a servant of the crown.[11]

The description of the episode regarding the monastic visitations of 1251 at first blush seems to be Elizabethan tabloid journalism at its best (or worst, as the case might be). It would be helpful to reproduce the notorious entry in its entirety, and then to analyze it.

> The same year the bishop of Lincolne visited the religious houses within his diocese, to vnderstand what rule was kept amongst them, vsing the matter somewhat strictlie (as they thought:) for he entred into the chambers of the moonks & searched their beds. And coming to the houses of the nuns, he went so néere as to cause their breasts to be tried, that he might vnderstand of their chaste liuings. In Lent following he was suspended by the pope, bicause he would not suffer an Italian that had no skill of the English toong to injoy a prebend in his church, which the pope had giuen to the same Italian.[12]

A number of observations can be made regarding the events depicted by Holinshed. First of all, Holinshed adds three significant words as an important editorial comment regarding the alleged strictness of Grosseteste's enforcement of monastic rules: "as they thought."[13] Perhaps he had come to the conclusion that many have regarding Matthew of Paris' (himself a monk) own editorial bent. Holinshed, after all, was writing in the same Tudor milieu that did not seem to regret or try to reverse the dissolution of the monasteries, even under Bloody Mary. In regard to the most egregious of events, that of the convent visitations, Holinshed seems to understand that in causing of the breasts of the nuns "to be tried,"[14] the bishop is ordering a fairly simple (albeit primitive and certainly embarrassing) procedure to see if any of the women might be nursing babies. It might also be suggested that the verb construction "to be tried," rather than "to try," could well imply, because of its ambiguity, that Grosseteste was present not as "trier" but as witness to the trying. In any case, Holinshed does not seem to add any editorial content in this context, though there was ample opportunity to do so if he had been scandalized in any way. Perhaps the last thing that might be said about the quote is that it appears in the same paragraph as the bishop of Lincoln's refusal to accept as prebend in his diocese an unqualified candidate, not because he was an Italian, but because he could not speak English and therefore not exercise properly the responsibilities of his office. (It is known from other documentation that the candidate's main qualification seemed to be that he was the pope's nephew.)[15] Holinshed duly notes that this resistance caused Grosseteste to be suspended from his office.

Holinshed also records that the bishop attempted to have all beneficed men in his diocese become priests, presumably because that was the way it was supposed to be, and also to meet the needs of parishioners when the number of priests was in short supply (an issue which the chronicler treats in the next paragraph, in fact).[16] But again the bishop's efforts were frustrated because, according to Holinshed, "they had purchased a license from Rome, to remaine at the Vniversities for certaine yeares, without taking the order of préesthood upon them."

But perhaps the most conclusive evidence concerning the Elizabethan's real regard for Grosseteste comes in the form of his death notice, drawn nearly verbatim from Matthew Paris, and clearly in his view one of the major events of the year 1253:

> This year died Richard Witz the bishop of Chichester, a man of great vertue and singular knowledge. Also that famous clearke Robert Grosted bishop of Lincolne departed this life on the day of S. Denise in the night, at his manor of Bugdon, whose learning coupled with vertue and vprightnesse of life wan to him perpetuall commendation. He was a manifest blamer of pope and king, a reproouer of prelats, a corrector of moonks, a director of preests, an instructor of clearkes, a susteinor of scholers, a preacher to the people, a persecutor of incontinent liuers, a diligent searcher of the scriptures, a contemnor and a verie mallet of such strangers as sought preferment in this realme by the popes prouisions: in housekeeping liberall, in corporall refection plentifull, and in ministring spirituall food, deuout and godlie affected: in his bishoplike office diligent, reverend, and neuer wearied.[17]

Thus far the obituary follows Matthew of Paris fairly closely, with the exception of Holinshed's and his successors' editorializing comment concerning "strangers" seeking preferment. But more important than this is the way that the chroniclers go on, now in their own words:

> A singular example of a bishop, speciallie in those daies, and at whose life our reformed bishops may fetch light to abandon their darkenesse, and to amend that which is amisse in them, sith
>
> Validiora sunt exempla quam precepta,
> Et plenius docemur vita quam verbo.[18]

Not only, then, does Holinshed not seem to bear any responsibility for the diminishing of Grosseteste's reputation, he clearly holds it up as a model life for a reforming bishop. It is fair to say, in fact, that in the entries prior to the sixteenth century in this 1586 edition of the *Chronicles*, there seem to be no other such panegyrics comparable to that awarded Grosseteste.

Why then does Grosseteste at times seem to lapse into a kind of obscurity? One part of the answer lies in that which has been already suggested, the fact that at least in the university community, elements of Grosseteste's writings (as well as that of the products of many other fine medieval intellects) were simply no longer fashionable. Another part of the answer may, however, lie within the attitudes of Holinshed himself and of the turbulent times in which he lived.

The net effect of Henry VIII's break with Rome is not to be undervalued. Monasticism for all intents and purposes vanished, along with a variety of other medieval institutions. The chantries suffered their demise under Edward VI, and the central doctrines of the mass were metamorphosed in the prayerbooks into deliberate linguistic ambiguity sometimes described by the term "charitable suppositions." But one institution that did not disappear was that of the episcopacy. Unlike their Stuart cousins, the Tudors were not yet faced with a large-scale opposition to episcopal polity. Rather, the Tudor monarchs' main problem vis-a-vis the bishops seemed to lie in their compliance (or lack thereof) with the objectives of royal policy over against their own god-given authority. Peter Brooks, in his essay on primitive protestantism, delineates very carefully the tradition of "sound Biblical scholarship and pastoral concern" that lay in nearly unbroken succession from Cranmer to Grindal in the sixteenth century.[19] That was a dynamic time for the Church in England, and her bishops were certainly not by any measure static men. It might be argued, then, that the Elizabethans of late sixteenth-century England had before them as intriguing and interesting an assortment of ecclesiastical figures as had any generation previous to their own.

In reading Patrick Collinson's life of Grindal, it is striking how many parallels there are to the career of Grosseteste. They were both known for their erudition. They were both benefactors of learning: Grosseteste to Oxford and Grindal to Cambridge. They were both supporters of preaching, and competent pastors. They were both rigorous in the enforcement of episcopal supervision. Both were willing to challenge higher authority regardless of consequences when the integrity of their offices are at stake, and both are known for making startling speeches in defense of their conduct: in the case of Grosseteste the ironic "as an obedient son I disobey"[20] and Grindal's "Bear with me, I beseech you, Madam, if I choose rather to offend your earthly majesty, than to offend the heavenly majesty of God," coupled with the well-known "Remember, madam, that you are a mortal creature."[21] And ultimately both did suffer the consequences of their actions -- Grosseteste being suspended by Pope Innocent IV, and Grindal by the *de facto* pope, Elizabeth herself.

But does Holinshed's *Chronicle*, now hopefully absolved of any guilt regarding the lessening of Grosseteste's reputation, demonstrate, perhaps, any kind of consciousness of this parallel view? The eulogy for Grindal, entered in the year 1583 might be offered as evidence:

> Edmund Grindal doctor of divinitie archbishop of Canturburie deceased at Croidon in Surrie on the sixt daie of July, and was there buried. This good man in his time was so studious, that his booke was his bride, his studie his bridechamber, wherevpon he spent both his eiesight, his strength, and his health, and therefore might verie well not actiuelie but passiuelie be named as (he was) Grindall; for he groond himself euen to his grave by mortification. Of whome much might be spoken for others imitation (sith the vse of the historie, is to instruct succeeding ages) but this shall suffice, that as his learning and vertue were inseparable comanions: so the reward of both is the good name he hath left behind him as a monument perpetuall, bicause vertue was the found of the same; according to the true saieng of the late poet importing no lesse:
>
> Virtutis merces eadem & labor, illa tropheum est,
> Solaque dat nigrae vincere mortis iter:
> Nam nisi virtutis quaeratur gloria factis,
> Omnis in extremos est abitura rogos.[22]

The parallels between the treatment of Grosseteste and Grindal would seem to be self-evident, even down to the little Latin verse at the end. And it is not here the purpose to debate or compare the intellectual stature of the two bishops, as it seems certain that Grosseteste was by far the more original and powerful thinker. But there is on the part of the chronicler a strong equivalency created, in the sense of a positive perception of both as exemplary reforming bishops. Unfortunately, even the chronicle as a means of preserving and transmitting a person's reputation was becoming increasingly less viable. D. R. Woolf has demonstrated recently that it was rapidly falling into disfavor as a literary form.[23] Given the hostility of the seventeenth century to bishops and the anti-clerical rationalism of the eighteenth century, it is a wonder that Grosseteste's reputation survived at all.

Grosseteste never did disappear, then. But if one were to agree with Southern that Holinshed's view determines the great bishop's place in English ecclesiastical history, it would have to be on the fact that the chronicler saw this lone voice crying in the wilderness of the thirteenth century as being blended into a rising sixteenth-century chorus for reform.

Notes

[1] Richard W. Southern, *Robert Grosseteste: The Growth of an English Mind in Medieval Europe* (London: 1986), p. 21.

[2] Cf. James Kelsey McConica, *English Humanists and Reformation Politics under Henry VIII and Edward VI* (Oxford, 1965), pp. 76-77.

[3] J. H. Srawley, *Robert Grosseteste, Bishop of Lincoln (1235-1253)* (Lincoln, 1966), p. 30.

[4] Robert Grosseteste, *De cessatione legalium*, ed. Richard C. Dales and Edward B. King, Auctores Britannici Medii Aevi 7 (London, 1986), pp. xviii, xx.

[5] Srawley, p. 30.

[6]6. J. F. W. Hill, "The Tomb of Robert Grosseteste with an Account of its Opening in 1782," *Robert Grosseteste, Scholar and Bishop*, ed. D. A. Callus (London, 1955), p. 247.

[7] Ibid., p. 248.

[8] Southern, p. 29.

[9] Cf. S. Harrison Thomson, *The Writings of Robert Grosseteste* (Cambridge, 1940).

[10] Raphael Holinshed, *The Third Volume of Chronicles*, edition of 1586, p. 378. Cf. also 2 Tim. 3.15.

[11] Holinshed, p. 418.

[12] Ibid, pp. 421-22.

[13] Ibid., p. 421.

[14] Ibid.

[15] Srawley, p. 25.

[16] Holinshed, p. 424.

[17] Ibid, p. 430.

[18] Ibid.

[19] Peter Newman Brooks, "The Principle and Practice of Primitive Protestantism in Tudor England: Cranmer, Parker and Grindal as Chief Pastors, 1535-1577," *Reformation Principle and Practice*, ed. Peter Newman Brooks (London, 1980), p. 132.

[20] Cf. Srawley, pp. 25-26.

[21] Patrick Collinson, *Archbishop Grindal, 1519-1583, The Struggle for a Reformed Church* (Berkeley, 1979), p. 244.

[22] Holinshed, pp. 505-6.

[23] D. R. Woolf, "Genre into Artifact: The Decline of the English Chronicle in the Sixteenth Century," *The Sixteenth Century Journal* 19 (1988), 321-54.

Part 2

MEDIEVAL INTELLECTUAL LIFE

Canonistic Determinations of the Stages of Childhood

Glenn M. Edwards

Thinkers in the western world have traditionally imposed an order upon human development, dividing life spans into three, four, five, seven, nine, or ten parts. Hesiod provides perhaps the earliest example of the hebdomadal division (that is commonly believed to have been so basic to medieval thought) when he wrote that children under the age of seven should not receive a literary education.[1] Franz Boll noted that the Greeks of the Classical Age divided life into seven stages corresponding to the planets, and he noted further that at the end of the Middle Ages, a belief in the sevenfold schedule of human development became popular as part of a growing desire to find harmony in the universe.[2]

But between the ancient world and the world of the Reformation lay an era not entirely given over to such schemes of human life. The Middle Ages are popularly considered to have been intellectually bookish and monk-ridden, but this study will show that when canonists and other ecclesiastical writers determined the end of the age of childhood, they were following not tradition, but nature.

Following Aristotle's *De anima*,[3] western thinkers commonly pursued a threefold division: youth, maturity, and old age. In the *Rhetoric*[4] he notes that youth is marked by strong but fickle passions, old age by the opposite of these youthful characteristics, and maturity by a combination of these two states. Certainly, no one could argue with this almost tautological proposition, and it would be surprising only to learn that the question never advanced past this point.

One idea of a seven-part division of human life was transmitted by Augustine to Isidore of Seville, both of whom were important sources for the later canonists. Augustine at one point divided the history of the world into six ages, and compared these to the six ages of the human life.[5] Elsewhere he used the seven-part scheme to note the correspondences among the six ages of man, the six ages of the world, and the six days of creation.[6] Admittedly, this is a bookish approach. Isidore notes in his *Liber numerorum*[7] that there are seven "year-weeks" in the human life, but in his *Differentiarum*[8] he follows Augustine's six ages. Isidore's treatment of the topic in his *Etymologies* lists the six ages of man as "infantia, pueritia, adolescentia, iuventus, gravitas atque senectus" and then sets three of these stages into seven-year periods: *infantia* to seven years, *pueritia* ("id est pura et necdum ad generandum apta") to fourteen, *adolescentia* ("ad gignendum adulta") to age twenty-eight, *iuventus* to forty-eight, *gravitas* between fifty and seventy, followed by *senectus* and death.[9]

The stages of childhood are thus three. Infancy, the first, extends from birth to age seven, which is the time of second dentition. (Isidore notes that infancy is so called because the *infans* cannot *fari*, "speak," because his teeth are not well formed.) The hebdomad then skips to age fourteen, when adolescence begins, and to the beginning of the stage of youth at age twenty-eight, after fourteen years of adolescence. The *juventus* lives between the ages of twenty-eight and fifty. This is the best age of a man's life, says the Venerable Bede in the early eighth century, and the age at which Adam was created.[10]

Bede himself follows a seven-part division of human history,[11] but the ages of man is not one of the six kinds of hebdomads he lists in his *De temporum ratione*.[12]

Later, in chapter 25 of *De temporum ratione*, Bede says that there is a scheme of life based on the four humors. Just as spring is moist and hot like air, so is childhood. Youth is like summer, hot and dry. Autumn and maturity are cold and wet, like water; and old age is dry and cold like winter. (The bodily humors have their counterparts to these, of course, which would have made the case all the more compelling.)

It is possible that this division goes back to Pythagorean number mysticism, and it certainly is an old and a scientific approach to the human life span. But, as will be seen, the canonists did not follow this approach because they were following their observations of nature more than the dictates of ancient or medieval medical theory.

In his penitential[13] Bede points out that a confessor must distinguish between rich and poor, and bright and dull, between infants, boys, youths, adolescents and the aged.[14] Adolescents are those who can copulate, and a *parvulus*, a word generally synonymous with *infans*, can be punished for fornication. This is an odd juxtaposition, that of an infant with the ability to sin. Perhaps Bede here means the word to indicate a boy (*puer*) of small stature, since he uses the word elsewhere as an adjective.[15] But the penance prescribed is relatively light, forty days, so perhaps what Bede had in mind was some form of childish sexual play.

The late Carolingian writer Rabanus Maurus lists six ages of man, including infancy to age seven and *pueritia* to age fourteen. (Following Isidore, he notes this as the age when one is pure and not suited for generation.) Then comes adolescence to age twenty-eight, the age "ad gignendum adulta." The time between the end of *pueritia* and the time of senility are the only two ages that Rabanus defines biologically rather than in terms of years only. Senility begins after the time of *gravitas*, a transitional age between that of the *iuventus* and the *senex*, and it lasts until death.[16]

In his book on the oblation of boys, Rabanus gives several clues to what he sees as the nature and capabilities of the different stages of childhood. Infants, for example, are in cradles and seem to be no different from *parvuli*. Infants, and those in *pueritia* can be oblated to the service of God. Isaac was a *puer* at the time of his near-sacrifice by Abraham, as was Jesus at the age of twelve when he spoke with the doctors in the temple.[17]

In the twelfth century, Hugh of St. Victor failed to distinguish between infants and *pueri*. *Parvuli*, he says, can be baptized though they have no free will or faith.[18] In dealing with the question of why the sin of the first man is imputed to his posterity, Hugh says that the original sin was disobedience and that this disobedience is reborn in all. But he goes on to say that it is not apparent that *pueri* are disobedient because nothing has ever been commanded of them. He sensibly asks how, if one is unable to use reason, can he be called obedient or disobedient.[19] Hugh seems to have been writing only of children under the age of seven, and there is nothing unusual or particularly remarkable in what he says except for his use of the word *puer* where one would expect *infans* or *parvulus*.

Alan of Lille is part of the generation that followed Hugh's. His *Liber penitentialis* indicates that *pueri* are marked by an inability to form words well[20] and by lasciviousness. Alan also says that *pueritia* is the most eminent of all the imbecilities of life. *Pueri* cannot walk, he says, they stammer when they speak, and cannot chew solid food.[21] Here Alan ascribes to *pueri* the characteristics that Isidore, Rabanus, and especially the writers who follow after Alan would want to ascribe to infants.

Albertus Magnus followed the fourfold division favored by Bede and others in the more scientific tradition of the Middle Ages. Like them, he defined the stage of a human life in biological terms that were, in fact, more philosophical than observational, in Albertus's case defining the stages as those when substance and power accumulate, when they stand still, when power declines, and finally when substance declines.

There were many answers, then, among the earlier, pre-canonist writers to the question of when childhood or adolescence ended. One could follow the scheme of Aristotle or the Pythagoreans that came down through Bede and Albertus or, if one wished, one could follow the sevenfold scheme found in Ptolemy's *Tetrabiblos*.[22] The writers of the age of the canonists thus had available to them many sorts of divisional schemes, some very logically or philosophically precise, but none that would help a canon lawyer very much at all.[23]

The two great canonical collections prior to Gratian's are those of Ivo of Chartres and Burchard of Worms. They offer a wealth of evidence drawn from instances that deal with the stages of childhood and the way canonists determined them.

Ivo's *Decretum* contains canons that use the words *parvulus* and *infans* interchangeably[24] and adjectivally.[25] *Parvuli* are characterized by a lack of free will due to their inability to reason. They alone can live without sin and are assured of heaven, but only if they die after baptism (and, presumably, are still in infancy). They are incapable of belief or confession of faith, but should, like the sick, be given the Eucharist if they are in danger of death.[26] Infants or the insane (*furiosi*) should not be punished, but infants or *pueri* who eat worms, scabs, lice, or excrement should be beaten. (This last comes from Bede's penitential and seems to be a negative reinforcement rather than a punishment for sin.) Neither *impuberes* nor the insane could perjure themselves since they have not the ability.[27]

Ivo deals also with the matter of oblates, and it is here that are found some details in the ages of children that may help more precisely measure the stages of childhood perceived by the canonists. He tells the story of a certain Lambert who was oblated between the ages of eight and eleven by his father, and he put on the cowl "extra omnem voluntatem illius." He was held in the monastery until the bishop inquired into the matter and decided that Lambert should be released from the monastery and restored to his share of the family inheritance. It does not tell the age at which Lambert was released by the bishop, but he was likely to have been past puberty. Ivo declares elsewhere that a son or daughter oblated before age seven can leave the monastery upon reaching puberty.[28]

Burchard of Worms's *Decretum* has little to say about the ages of children that cannot already be found in either Bede or Ivo. Bede's injunction to a confessor to discriminate between "infants, boys, youths, adolescents, and the old" is here, as is Bede's injunction against eaters of worms and excrement.[29] Ivo said that those girls who freely take the veil before age twelve cannot leave the convent if they later took their vows "in a stronger age." Burchard clarifies this by defining the stronger age as adolescence.[30]

Gratian, too, observes that *pueri* do not believe "with their own will" and are unable to do penance for sin.[31] This is because it is not necessary. Sins are not to be imputed to anyone after baptism, neither child nor adult, unless their age is capable of reason. A girl under twelve is subject to the will of her father, but after that age she can choose a religious life if she wishes, and her parents have not the power to stop her. Likewise, a child oblated as an infant could leave the monastery upon reaching puberty. Gratian also says that a *puer* should not enter a harsh monastic rule until age eighteen.[32]

Rufinus of Bologna's *Summa decretorum*, written about 1157, indicates that the age of seven is the time when there is a change in the status of children, for that is the age at which they attain the capacity for deceit, the *capax doli*.[33] Interestingly enough, it is this capacity that makes them eligible to testify in court: "If they are able to speak, and particularly after they have become seven years old, they are able to speak for themselves. In the seventh year of their age, children are able to think, speak truth, confess, and deny. And therefore they have been baptized and they recite the creed and answer questions for themselves."[34]

Magister Rolandus Bandinelli, later Pope Alexander III, said that children are in the power of their parents to age twelve or fourteen, and that the bishop should question oblates during their first year of puberty to see if they wished to remain in the monastery.[35] And Vincent of Beauvais made several statements on children's ages and abilities that by now seem familiar. In his book on the education of the sons of nobility, written about 1244, Vincent notes that those in new infancy are not fit for reading or comprehension and agrees with Ovid that *pueri* are fit to be shaped and governed.[36] The age of *pueritia* is the age for schooling. After treating the education of boys, he turns to that of adolescents--a word seldom encountered in canon law--and tells that they must be disciplined because they now have the use of reason and are prone to luxury, dissolution, and lasciviousness.[37]

This is not to say that adolescents are those newly arrived at the age of reason. Those are *pueri*. Adolescents are those who are now able to "join puberty to reason," and trouble consequently arises. Note that adolescents are not *impuberes*. Vincent goes on to say that boys between seven and fourteen have reason, but it is only when the *capax doli* is joined to the generative ability that greater and more exacting discipline is necessary. (Georges Duby's article on the aristocratic youths of northwestern France in the twelfth century leads one to believe that their families regularly sent them out on the tournament circuit to get them out of the neighborhood until they settled down.[38]) The important point is not, of course, the antics of adolescents, but rather that adolescence is defined by generative ability rather than by age. Vincent notes that it begins around age fourteen, but the attainment of that age is not the criterion.

The decretalist Hostiensis, writing shortly after Vincent, said that children were punished not spiritually but bodily, and this went lightly with them. He adds that there was no culpability in infants under the age of seven.[39] He also said that there were three ages of childhood: infancy from birth to age seven, impuberty from seven to twelve or fourteen depending upon sex, and puberty from that age to the *plena pubertas* at age eighteen. Puberty was determined by the appearance of the body (the growth of a beard and the appearance of pubic hair), the attainment of the proper age, and the *rei evidentiam*.[40] Hostiensis felt that the attainment of the approximate age was an unreliable guide; the *habitus corporis* was the only sure indication.[41]

All these ecclesiastical determinations of the ages of children have one thing substantially in common. Leaving aside the minor differences in vocabulary and the shifting age limits of adolescence, one finds that *pueri* are defined biologically. This is not the case in some other medieval sources.

Ducange defines a *puer* as a dependent man (*homo famulus*) of any age, as a servant, lesser cleric, poor scholar, and so on. Of the fifteen definitions he gives, only one, "oblates of tender years educated in the cloister," refers definitely to a prepubescent state rather than to a state of dependency. Interestingly enough, this definition is given last of all. As far as Ducange is concerned, the word *puer* denotes dependency far more often than it does childhood.

Paul Guilhiermoz says in his *Essai sur l'origine de la Noblesse en France au Moyen Age*[42] that the word *puer* has several meanings. First of all, it means *enfans*, young people, and "young people of a certain age." It also means domestic (particularly royal) servants. The Vandals chose a champion to fight for them in single combat against the champion of another tribe. Both champions are called *pueri*. Guilhiermoz cites the use of *pueri* by Gregory of Tours to denote scholars, by the *Chronicle of Fredegar* to describe the personal troops of Belisarius, and by Willibald to describe the companions and body guards of St. Boniface. He thinks this usage may be inspired by the Bible.[43]

The Bible does use the word *puer* to describe a servant perhaps a bit more often than to describe a prepubescent male. In 1 Kings 25 the troops of David are invariably *pueri*, and in 4 Kings 4.1-37 Elisha and his servant (*puer*) restore to life the child (*puer*) of the Shunammite woman. *Puer*, meaning boy, and *puer*, meaning servant, alternate so rapidly that one can be driven dizzy. Moses was a *puer* in the bullrushes (Ex. 2.7), and Joshua was a *puer* when he helped Moses lead the Hebrews toward Mount Sinai (Ex. 33.1).

It seems likely that if the canonists had been relying heavily upon the Bible for their vocabulary of the stages of childhood, they would have broadened their definition of *puer* to include the concept of dependency rather than of age. Furthermore, there are quite a number of other elements in the Bible that support divisions the canonists did not use. The parable of the vineyard supports a fivefold scheme of life, and the watches of the liturgical night supported a fourfold scheme. Gregory the Great derived analogies from these, but the canonists did not follow this particular set of leads.[44]

But not only in the theoretical works of the canonists does one find a *puer* defined primarily as a boy rather than as a servant. The more practical works, such as the synodal statutes of Great Britain and Ireland, contain only one use of the word *puer* that could possibly mean a servant rather than a child.[45] But even that evidence is doubtful, and the weight of evidence is in favor of biology. The Statutes of Coventry (1224-1237) contain a treatise on the seven deadly sins. The trouble with drunkenness, a form of gluttony, is that "drunkards often drown themselves, are killed, kill others, burn their houses, themselves, and their own *pueros*." There is nothing in the canon to deny the possibility that *pueri* here means servants, but the very next sentence notes that parents often suffocate their own sons.[46]

The Roman Law tends to obscure the difference between a *puer* and a *filius*; particularly in matters of wardship, care, and tutelage. Clyde Pharr's translation of the Theodosian Code even states this outright.[47] The translator saw fit to equate *puer* with *filius*, and the distinction in the Roman Law is indeed possible since it seems that in this case, a *puer* is anyone under paternal power or under the guardianship of a tutor or curator. Bracton wrote in his commentary on the English Law that the insane cannot stipulate, nor can an infant or one just out of infancy. These, Bracton points out, do not differ greatly from lunatics.[48] The civil lawyers based their concept of boyhood upon a notion of legal competence rather than upon biology. (Biology does, of course, enter into the matter.)

The canonist Hostiensis knew this well and felt that the *habitus corporis* was the only sure indication of puberty. The attainment of the proper age was a minor indication at best (see above). He was vehement, in fact, against mere age as an indication of the advent of puberty, and the occasion of assuming the rights, privileges, and duties of those who were no longer in *pueritia*.[49] When the canonists determined that the age of *pueritia* was twelve for girls and fourteen for boys, they did so not because they were following classical, patristic, or biblical practice, nor because they wished to determine a definite chronological age of either culpability for sin or freedom from parental power. Had they been following medical theory, their writings would be reminiscent of chapter 35 of Bede's *De temporum ratione*. The canonists were simply following nature.

But "following nature" is a tricky business in the Middle Ages because the scientific tradition of the time (that is, the scheme for understanding nature) was so often mixed in with astronomy. Consider, for example, Bede's relation of the seasons and bodily humors to the ages of man. An examination of the *Tetrabiblos* shows the same sort of principle the canonists used, that of looking to nature to determine the condition of the body. But the difference is great. Ptolemy notes that the moon rules a child to age four, an age when a human is quick, changeable, supple, and moist. For the next ten years the child is ruled by Mercury, learning to speak, becoming intelligent and rational, and so on through the remainder of the planets. Venus rules for eight years, "corresponding in number to her own period," the sun for nineteen, Mars for fifteen years, "equal to his own period," Jupiter "for the space of his own period, twelve years," and Saturn ruled for the rest of life.[50] But even though this scheme was supposedly based on observation, and an astrologer could tell the life-stage of a person by an examination of his *habitus corporis*, to use the phrase from Hostiensis, they nevertheless still based their judgments upon a divisional scheme extraneous to the person being examined. Ultimately, they drew their conclusions *a priori* from the astronomy of their time rather than from an observation of the life around them.

There have been some studies made of the relation of nutritional and other factors to the onset of menarche. One such study of the medical literature of the Middle Ages by Darrell W. Amundsen and Carol Jean Diers[51] supports a study published earlier by J. B. Post, who detected for the Middle Ages "an age at menarche equivalent, and an age at menopause not dissimilar, to those apparent in the mid-twentieth century."[52] When canonists said that puberty began around twelve for girls, then, they were probably right. But they knew enough not to depend upon the body's acquiescence to the dictates of theoreticians.

Notes

[1] *Hesiod: The Homeric Hymns and Homerica*, trans. Hugh G. Evelyn-White (Cambridge [Mass.], 1904), p. 75.

[2] Franz Boll, *Sternglaube und Sterndeutung: Die Geschichte und das Wesen der Astrologie*, 5th revised ed. by H. G. Gundel, (Stuttgart, 1966), pp. 65-66, 74.

[3] "De partibus, quos diversi sensus in vita animalium agunt . . . . Quod enim natum est, debet necessario crescere, maturitatem attingere, et tabescere," *Aristotelis tractatus de anima graece et latine* 3.12 (434a, lines 24-25), ed. Paulus Siwek, (Rome, 1965), p. 231.

[4] *Rhetoric* 2.12-14, in Aristotle, *The "Art" of Rhetoric*, trans. John Henry Freese (Cambridge [Mass.], 1926), pp. 247-57.

[5] *De diversis questionibus LXXXIII* 1.43 (PL 40:43).

[6] *De Genesi contra Manichaeos* 1.23 (PL 34:190-93). Augustine here adds a seventh age to human life, the resurrection of the body, corresponding to the seventh day on which God rested. See also J. A. Burrow, *The Ages of Man: A Study in Medieval Writing and Thought* (Oxford, 1986), for a very useful survey, though one heavily weighted to the literary, of the ancient and medieval categories of human life spans.

[7] *Liber numerorum* 8 ("De septenario numero,") (PL 83:188).

[8] *Liber differentiarum* 2.19 (PL 83:81-82).

[9] Isidore of Seville, *Etymologiarum sive Originum libri XX* 11.2 ("De aetatibus hominum,") ed. W. M. Lindsay, vol. 2 (Oxford, 1911, reprinted ed. 1966), unpaginated. See also PL 91:21.

[10] Bede, *Hexaemeron* 1 (PL 91:36-38).

[11] *De temporum ratione* 10 ("De hebdomada aetatum saeculi,") ed. Charles W. Jones, *Bedae opera de temporibus* (Cambridge [Mass.], 1943), pp. 201-2.

[12] Ibid. 7 ("De hebdomada,") in Jones, pp. 195-98. Those he lists are the days of creation, the days of the week, the planets, Pentecost, the Great Sabbath, and the Jubilee.

[13] Bede, *De remediis peccatorum*, PL 94:567-76.

[14] Ibid., cols. 570: "Si parvulus vi oppressus talia patitur, xl dies poeniteat, vel psalmis vel continentia castigetur."

[15] Ibid., cols. 527, 569.

[16] Rabanus Maurus, *De universo* 7.1 (PL 111:179).

[17] Rabanus Maurus, *Liber de oblatione puerorum* (PL 107:419-40, especially 419, 422, 430, 432).

[18] Hugh of St. Victor, *Summa sententiarum* 5.5 (PL 176:130).

[19] Ibid., (PL 176:106-7).

[20] *Liber poenitentialis*, PL 210:281-82. The latter example seems to contradict the etymology of *puer* and *pura*, incidentally; much work could be done on medieval ideas of childish innocence.

[21] Ibid., col. 284.

[22] Claudius Ptolemy, *Tetrabiblos* 4.10, ed. and trans. F. E. Robbins (Cambridge [Mass.], 1971), pp. 437-59.

[23] The same point is made by Burrow (p. 34): "It can by no means be assumed that such numbers bear any relation to the social or biological relations of the time [in which they are formulated]. Very often they are based upon numerological considerations, such as the concept of the 'year-week' or seven-year cycle, according to which seven, fourteen, twenty-eight, thirty-five, and so on, become critical years; and such considerations can, of course, produce many different results."

[24] Ivo of Chartres, *Decretum* 1.150, 222; 3.253; 10.27; et cetera (PL 161, passim).

[25] Ibid. 1.178, 243, et cetera.

[26] Ibid. 1.30, 41, 178; 2.20.

[27] Ibid. 13.86, 93; 15.96.

[28] Ibid. 6.356; 7.15.

[29] *Burchardi Wormaciensis episcopi decretum libri XX* 19.9, 84 (PL 140:980).

[30] Ivo, *Decretum* 8.98.

[31] Gratianus, *Decreti* 1.15.1.3 (PL 187).

[32] Ibid. 2.20.2.2 and 2.20.1.5 (Palea--Pope Gregory to Anthemium, ep. 48).

[33] Rufinus, *Summa decretorum*, in *Die 'Summa decretorum' des Magister Rufinus*, ed., Heinrich Singer (Paderborn, 1902), p. 381.

[34] Ibid. 3.4.74 (pp. 565-66).

[35] Roland Bandinelli, *Summa* 22.1.2, in *Die 'Summa magistri Rolandi,' nachmals Papstes Alexander III*, ed. Frederick Thaner (Innsbruck, 1874).

[36] Vincent of Beauvais, *De eruditione filiorum nobilium*, ed. Arpad Steiner (Cambridge [Mass.], 1938), pp. 3, 79-80.

[37] Ibid., p. 135.

[38] Reprinted in *Lordship and Community in Medieval France*, ed. and trans. Frederick L. Cheyette (New York, 1968), pp. 198-209.

[39] Hostiensis, "De delictis puerorum," in *Summa aurea* 22.9.5 (Venice, 1574).

[40] Ibid., col. 1268.

[41] *Summa* (Lyons, 1537), fol. 198b.

[42] Paris, 1902, reprint Burt Franklin.

[43] Ibid., pp. 52-54.

[44] Burrow, p. 67.

[45] This is to the best of my knowledge, and I have searched every canon. Frederick M. Powicke and Christopher R. Cheney, eds., *Councils and Synods, with Other Documents Relating to the English Church* (Oxford, 1964).

[46] Ibid., p. 220.

[47] *The Theodosian Code and Novels and the Sirmondian Constitutions*, ed. and trans. Clyde Pharr (Princeton, 1952), p. 103 n. 1.

[48] Samuel F. Thorne, trans., *Bracton on the Laws and Customs of England* (Cambridge [Mass.], 1969), 2:286. Bracton is citing Justinian's *Institutes* in this instance.

[49] *Summa* (Lyons, 1537), fol. 198b.

[50] Ptolemy, *Tetrabiblos*, pp. 444-57.

[51] Darrell W. Amundsen and Carol Jean Diers, "The Age of Menarche in Medieval England," *Human Biology* 45 (1973), 363-69. Note especially: "The ages for menarche given by the classical authors are not parroted by the medieval authors. Also, in the realm of superstition, there is virtually no evidence of hebdomadism, so popular during the classical period" (p. 368).

[52] J. B. Post, "Ages of Menarche and Menopause: Some Medieval Authors," *Population Studies* 25 (1971), 83-87, see especially p. 87.

Hugh of Amiens: An Abelardian Against Abelard

Gunar Freibergs

After Peter Abelard had been condemned by the Synod of Sens, and had stopped at Cluny while on his way to Rome, a new participant appeared in the ranks of those aligned against him: Hugh of Amiens, the archbishop of Rouen.[1] Unlike William of St. Thierry and Bernard of Clairvaux, however, whose attacks on Abelard's scholarship had been open, Hugh chose to counter Peter's newly published *Apologia contra Bernardum*[2] indirectly by persuading Thomas of Morigny to compose a *Disputatio adversus dogmata Petri Abaelardi*.[3] Thus, although it is clear that the archbishop was antagonistic, the extent to which he may have been informed about Peter's heresies, or the degree to which he would have known, understood and shared the specific objections raised by Abelard's adversaries has remained unexplored. Nor is it known whether he had been motivated to join the opposition out of some doctrinal or philosophical contention, or merely as a fellow traveler.

At about the time of Abelard's demise (1142), however, Hugh published his *Tractatus in hexaemeron*,[4] a commentary on the creation myth of Genesis.[5] Since works of this type addressed such questions as the nature of the deity, the relationship between the supernatural world and the natural, and the creation of matter, the earth and man, an examination of Hugh's *Tractatus* might possibly furnish clues about where he stood on some of the very issues for which Abelard had been brought before the synod.

The medieval Latin hexameron had been developed by Bede, who forsook the elaborate and highly allegorical explanations of Augustine in favor of a more literal and scientifically based exposition. Before the middle of the twelfth century that kind of exegesis reached new heights of scholarship when prominent *magistri* introduced further innovations. Peter Abelard published his own *Expositio in hexameron*,[6] a work which mostly adhered to the traditional forms established by Augustine's *De Genesi ad litteram*,[7] but differed from it by offering naturalistic, grammatical, and Platonic expositions. The distinction for the potentially most controversial hexameron of the time, however, must go to the *Tractatus de sex dierum operibus* of Peter's contemporary, Thierry of Chartres (d. ca. 1156), in which the whole process of creation is presented "secundum phisicam et ad litteram"[8] in a way where God is responsible only for the initial creative act, everything else evolving from there through a series of natural causes.

Hugh's hexameron, by comparison, is aesthetically attractive but intellectually uninspiring. Written in seventy-six chapters of varying length, it was intended as a theological tractate on Adam's sin and the expulsion of mankind from the Garden of Eden. The first forty-two chapters cover the six days of creation. Since in an earlier work, the *Dialogi*, he had already delved into the mystic symbolism of the six days, in the hexameron Hugh turns to the pursuit of the allegorical and moral meanings.[9] Composed in ornate prose which often rhymes or breaks into leonine verse, filled with neologisms, parallelism, repetition, paranomasia, and flowing with elegance, it follows a monastic style which the nineteenth-century scholar P. Hébert characterized as *plus soignée*.[10]

Although Hugh's often poetic style does not facilitate the identification of his sources, it is nevertheless possible to detect the author's indebtedness to the standard hexameral writers of late antiquity. By far the bulk of his material has been appropriated liberally from Augustine's *De Genesi ad litteram*. But it is also possible to detect the influences of Ambrose of Milan, Gregory the Great and Bede. Of his contemporaries, Hugh mentions only a Cluniac brother, "Matheo, Albanesi episcopo," to whom he had dedicated the *Dialogi*, and Arnulf, bishop of Lisieux (a friend of Bernard of Clairvaux), to whom he was dedicating the *Tractatus in hexaemeron*.[11] Neither one appears to have had more than a passing interest in hexameral literature. It is, however, with respect to ideas which coincide with those expressed by the more progressive twelfth-century minds that Hugh's work takes on a particular significance. These subtle connections might be best perceived by taking a look at Thierry's explanation of the roles played by both God and nature in the creation of the world.

According to Thierry of Chartres, when God, as the efficient cause, created everything instantly *in principio*, in the first moment of time, this specifically meant that he produced the four elements of matter,[12] each imbued with its preexisting *natura*[13] and a *virtute operatrice*.[14] The elements, being *naturaliter*[15] an amorphous mass of primordial *materia informis*, are the material cause of everything that was to be formed and distinguished in the course of the subsequent six days. "And apart from these ways of creating corporeal creatures," Thierry concludes, "there can be no way left." After the initial act of creation, God becomes a spectator watching the universe unfold by its own inbuilt natural powers and causes.[16] Almost as an afterthought, Thierry adds: "De diuinitate pauca dicenda sunt."[17]

Thierry goes on to explain that whatever creative activity might still be going on, it is no different than what was happening during the initial week of creation:

> Whatever, therefore, is born or created after the sixth day, is not made by some new type of creation, but was allotted its substance in one of the aforesaid manners. Thus, therefore, God rested on the seventh day, that is, he did not devise any new method of creation: concord had been perfectly assigned to each of the elements,

> both with respect to its own properties and in relation to all the others. For even though he later created new wonders,[18] we nevertheless do not say that he employed a new method of creation. But we affirm that, in one of the aforesaid ways and from the seminal causes which he bestowed on the elements in the space of the six days, he produced whatever he later created and still creates.[19]

Thierry's case is clear: the creation of the six days took place through natural powers and seminal causes resident in the elements, and that is how any creativity continues still today.

Peter Abelard agreed with some parts of Thierry's argument, but took exception with others. In his own *Expositio in hexameron*, as Richard C. Dales has pointed out,[20] he not only concurred with Thierry in regarding nature as a self-sufficient system, but took the matter a step further. Thierry had spoken of powers and causes which functioned naturally. Abelard designates these with specific terms: the elemental power in nature is the *vis naturae*, and the causes are *causas naturales*.

> Today we require or attribute a power of nature (*vis naturae*) or natural causes (*causas naturales*) to effects in things. . . . we are accustomed to consider the power of nature, when these things have already been made in such a way that their nature or preparation would suffice to do anything at all without miracles. . . . Therefore we call nature the power of things which, conferred upon them from that first preparation, in giving rise to anything, is sufficient to bring it about.[21]

But in spite of this agreement on the natural power and causes by which nature recognizably functions, Abelard, as Dales has pointed out, "takes issue with some unnamed contemporary (probably Thierry of Chartres) on the necessity of providing a naturalistic explanation for all the details of creation."[22]

> Although today we require or attribute a power of nature or natural causes to effects in things, we should in no way do the same with regard to that prior work of God, when God's will alone had the efficacy of nature in creating or arranging those things, that is, during that work completed by God in those six days. . . . during those six days . . . his will alone had the power of nature in each action. . . . So let no one ask what natural power [brought those things about], when at that time only God's will, as has been said, possessed the power of nature.[23]

To Abelard not just the initial creation of matter, but also the subsequent creative activity of the six days, was the direct work of God. Only afterwards do the causes and powers of nature take over by themselves.

In taking up the subject of the creation in his own hexameron, Hugh of Amiens likewise recognizes that the elements possess certain natural properties and behave *naturaliter*.[24] And, like Thierry and Abelard, he enters into a discussion about *causas naturales*, which he further divides into superior and inferior causes:

> Truly, he implanted natural causes in these things which he made. From the superior causes derives the inevitability of things, from the inferior their possibility. By virtue of superior causes of things it is necessary [for a thing] to become whatever it is, by inferior causes it is possible to become what it is; . . . See, therefore, that by virtue of the superior cause, that is by the will of God, which is always free, it is necessary for all things to be made. But those which are made, because they proceeded from nothing, are subject to mutability. That which God prearranged in them to be made from them can, by virtue of their mutability, be made from them, although it is not by necessity.[25]

Here the *causae superiores* are the will of God, which created things as they had to be; the *causae inferiores* correspond to Abelard's *causae naturales* and *vis naturae*. Although the emphasis is somewhat different, as is the terminology, Hugh clearly sides with Abelard. In commenting on the creation of the firmament Abelard had stressed that "at that time only God's will . . . possessed the power of nature."[26] In glossing the same *lemma*, Hugh is emphatic in declaring that the composition, laws and order of nature must be perceived as existing "only by the will of God."[27] Clearly, on the subject of how God performed the work of the six days, and what part nature played in the entire process, Hugh follows the explanation offered by Abelard.

One of Abelard's tactics in his hexameron had been to utilize innovative arguments as evidence to support certain established truths. To illustrate that the Trinity is three persons in one, he offered an argument based on the grammatical structure of the Hebrew word *Elohim* (which he spells *Heloym*). Although he uses somewhat different vocabulary, nevertheless glossing the same *lemma* and following idea for idea and thought for thought, Hugh uses Abelard's argument as demonstrative of the unity of the Trinity.[28]

> Thereafter it is written by Moses: "God created." In Hebrew "elohim" is written in place of this word which we say "God." Among the Hebrews, truly, "elohim" is a plural word, but it is not possible to translate this idiom into the Latin language. Thus it is that among the Hebrews "bara elohim," if you translate it word for word, in Latin speech appears to say, contrary to usage, "gods created." Wherefore it is to be noted that the word "elohim" signifies God in the plural pronunciation, but that it cannot mean plural gods is determined by the added singular Hebrew word, which is "bara," which among the Latins is "[he] created." This Hebrew expression, thus correctly used, our priests piously defend, who preach to adore the trinity which is in simple unity, which their singular word added to the plural, that is "bara elohim," represents.[29]

These congruences between the thought of Abelard and Hugh of Amiens are significant. They are not, however, without an element of dissent. Concerning God's omnipotence, Abelard had argued that the deity does everything in the optimum manner, but that this he cannot exceed.[30] In commenting on the biblical passage which relates that after the creation of man God saw that everything was very good, Hugh takes issue with "some who think to deprive man of this singular benediction," and then goes on to assert in no uncertain terms that "God made everything better than the best." This can only be a veiled reference to Abelard.[31]

What is to be made of these correspondences and conflicts with the thought of Abelard? The agreement with Abelard on the details of the creation suggests that Hugh may have read some version of Peter's hexameron, or at least have heard about it. However, it seems ironic that at a time when he had aligned himself with the opposition the good archbishop should find anything of value in the works of a rational scholar such as Abelard, and one tinged with heresy at that. Hugh of Amiens (1080-1164) was a conservative cleric. The son of a noble Norman family, he had received his formative education from Anselm of Laon and subsequently taken his monastic vows at Cluny. His display of administrative talent had led to an appointment as prior of Lewes in England, and soon thereafter Henry I had made him abbot of Reading (1125). In his powerful office as archbishop of Rouen (1130-1164), Hugh enjoyed acquaintance with several kings and was much in demand as an arbitrator in the conflict between Stephen and Mathilda for the English crown. In the disputed papal election of 1130 Hugh had sided with Innocent II, but also acted as mediator between him and Anacletus. He appears to have been, then, not the kind of person who would be interested in academic pursuits, but rather an ambitious member of the clergy climbing the ladder of success within the ecclesiastical hierarchy. His monastic conservatism, authoritarian manner, reputation as a strict disciplinarian, support of Bernard of Clairvaux's opposition to rational enquiry into the meaning of scripture, and the polemical nature of his writings have caused Hugh to be regarded as a rigorist theologian and one of the most redoubtable twelfth-century champions of Church tradition.

It is uncertain when Hugh may have first encountered Abelard, or when he may have begun to oppose him. Since their ages were almost identical, it is possible that they may have first met while studying under Anselm of Laon. Also, Abelard's friend Peter the Venerable had been Hugh's abbot at Cluny; it is possible that Hugh and Peter may have been there at the same time. When Pope Innocent II came to northern France in 1131, he found in Hugh an energetic supporter. Bernard of Clairvaux and Peter Abelard were among those who met with the pontiff that year during his visit to the monastery of Morigny,[32] a celebrated occasion from which Hugh, as archbishop and supporter of the pontiff, could hardly have been absent. Hugh could, then, have had considerable contact with Abelard over the years. It has been suggested that Hugh's *Dialogi*, revised in 1130-1134, show traces of Abelard's influence, and on this basis Luscombe has counted him as a member of the school of Abelard.[33]

It appears puzzling, therefore, that in his hexameron Hugh would make no mention of Abelard nor condemn his teachings. Although the work is dedicated to Arnulf, bishop of Lisieux, a close friend of Bernard of Clairvaux, it contains no references to the controversy and engages in no polemics. In fact Hugh has obviously integrated some Abelardian material into his own commentary.

At this point it might be worth asking: if indeed Hugh had read Abelard's *Expositio* (presuming he had), did he know what he was reading, and did he understand it? Many of the surviving manuscripts of Abelard's hexameron make no mention of the author's name. Since this work had never been singled out by William of St. Thierry or Bernard of Clairvaux, it may not have been associated with the stigma of heresy. Yet a critical antagonist could have had a field day with Abelard's metaphor of the cosmic egg, which he uses to illustrate how the spirit of God performed the work of creation.[34] An informed person would also not have illustrated the difference between potential and actual existence by reference to a wax image, which Hugh does with apparent ignorance of the sensitivities which Abelard had aroused with a similar analogy.[35] His one specific criticism of Abelard, that God does make everything *bonus bona*, is of little consequence. Hugh of St. Victor had already taken that to task some years earlier; by the time that Hugh of Amiens did his writing it had the power of a cliché.[36]

Hugh, it would appear, may indeed have been a member of the "school of Abelard," as his espousal of the Abelardian ideas about the creation shows. But although these are to be found in Abelard's hexameron, Hugh need not have obtained them from that source. Peter's ideas about the creation, the *vis naturae*, and the name *Elohim* were not recent conceptions; they were available in his other writings long before he repeated them in the *Expositio in hexameron*. In his hexameron Hugh also espouses a sympathetic view toward women, arguing that woman, like man, was created in the image of God.[37] In the hexameron, by contrast, as Mary McLaughlin has pointed out, Peter expresses a much more traditional and negative attitude toward women, one which Hugh does not reflect.[38] It would appear, then, that at the time of Abelard's condemnation Hugh's knowledge of the master's thought must have been horribly out of date, meaning also that he would have possessed at best a superficial grasp of the current issues. That kind of an attitude places Hugh of Amiens squarely among those prelates at Sens who in the burping and belching aftermath of a hearty meal endorsed Bernard's condemnation of Abelard with a soporific "*'namus!*"[39]

Notes

[1] Eligius M. Buytaert, O.F.M., in the General Introduction to *Petri Abaelardi Opera Theologica*, ed. E. M. Buytaert, Corpus Christianorum Continuatio Mediaeualis 11 (Turnholt, 1969), pp. xi, 348.

[2] *Petri Abaelardi Apologia contra Bernardum*, critical text in op. cit., pp. 343-68.

[3] Thomas of Morigny's authorship of this work has been demonstrated by M. B. Carra de Vaux St. Cyr, "Disputatio catholicorum patrum aduersus dogmata Petri Abaelardi," *Revue des sciences*

philosophiques et théologiques 47 (1963), 205-20. See also E. M. Buytaert, "Thomas of Morigny and the 'Apologia' of Abelard," *Antonianum* 42 (1967), 31-53.

[4] Francis Lecomte, ed., "Un commentaire scripturaire du XIIe siècle, le *Tractatus in hexaemeron* de Hughes d'Amiens," *Archives d'histoire doctrinale et littéraire du moyen âge* 25 (1958), 227-94. For biographical information, see P. Hébert, "Un archévéque de Rouen au XIIe siècle: Hugues III d'Amiens (1130-1164)," *Revue des questions historiques* 64 (1898), 325-71; *Dictionnaire de théologie Catholique* s.v. "Hughes d'Amiens," by E. Vacandard; J. B. Hurry, *In Honour of Hugh of Boves* (Reading, 1911).

[5] For a history of the Latin hexameron, see Frank E. Robbins, *The Hexameral Literature: A Study of the Greek and Latin Commentaries on Genesis* (Chicago, 1912); Gunar Freibergs, "The Medieval Latin Hexameron from Bede to Grosseteste," unpublished Ph.D. dissertation (University of Southern California, 1981).

[6] Mary F. Romig, ed., "A Critical Edition of Peter Abelard's *Expositio in hexameron*," unpublished Ph.D. dissertation (University of Southern California, 1981); see also PL 178:731-84.

[7] So Augustinian, in fact, is Abelard's hexameron, that it has even been criticized for possessing very little if any originality; Leo Scheffczyk, *Schöpfung und Vorsehung*, Handbuch der Dogmengeschichte, no. 2, fasc. 2a (Freiburg, 1963), pp. 79-80. See, however, Romig, pp. xxvii-xxxv, for a more balanced assessment.

[8] *Tractatus de sex dierum operibus*, ed. Nikolaus M. Häring, in *Commentaries on Boethius by Thierry of Chartres and His School* (Toronto, 1971), pp, 553-57.

[9] *Tractatus in hexaemeron* 8 (p. 242): "Nunc autem in hoc opusculo nostro magis historiam exquirendo tractamus, quam sensus allegoricos seu morales attingamus"; translation mine.

[10] Hébert, p. 369.

[11] Hugh, *Tractatus*, dedicatory letter and chap. 39 (pp. 235, 263).

[12] Thierry, *Tractatus* 2-5 (pp. 555-57).

[13] Ibid. 38 (p. 571): "Prior . . . generatio rerum est eiusdem nature."

[14] Ibid. 29 (p. 567).

[15] Ibid. 24 (p. 566).

[16] Ibid. 5-17, 28 (pp. 557-62, 567).

[17] Ibid. 29 (p. 568).

[18] The reference here may be to God making the great fish which swallowed Jonah.

[19] Thierry, *Tractatus* 15-16 (pp. 561-62).

[20] "A Twelfth-Century Concept of the Natural Order," *Viator* 9 (1978), 182.

[21] "Ad quod primum respondeo nullatenus nos modo, cum in aliquibus rerum effectis vim naturae vel causas naturales requirimus vel assignamus, id nos facere secundum illam priorem dei operationem in constitutione mundi, ubi sola dei voluntas naturae efficatiam habuit in illis tunc creandis vel disponendis; sed tantum ab illa operatione dei vi. diebus illis completa. Deinceps vim nature pensare solemus, tunc videlicet rebus ipsis iam ita preparatis, ut ad quelibet sine miraculis facienda illa eorum constitutio vel preparatio sufficet. Unde illa que per miracula fiunt magis contra vel supra naturam quam secundum naturam fieri fatemur, cum ad illud scilicet faciendum nequaquam illa rerum preparatio prior sufficere posset, nisi quamdam vim novam rebus ipsis deus conferret, sicut et in illis vi. diebus faciebat, ubi sola eius voluntas vim nature obtinebat in singulis efficiendis. Que quidem si nunc quoque sicut tunc faceret, profecto contra naturam hec fieri dicerimus. Veluti si terra sponte sua sine seminario aliquo plantas produceret, vel bestias ex se, vel aqua volucres formaret. Naturam itaque dicimus vim rerum ex illa prima preparatione illis collatam, ad aliquod inde nascendum, hoc est efficiendum sufficientem"; ed. Romig, pp. 38-39 (cf. PL 178:749), translation mine. The concept of *vis naturae* occurs also in Abelard's *Logica 'Ingredientibus' in*

Categorias, ed. B. Geyer, *Beiträge zur Geschichte der Philosophie und der Theologie des Mittelalters* 21, part 1 (Münster i. W., 1919), p. 33; part 2 (Münster i. W., 1921), p. 298; *Dialectica*, ed. De Rijk, ibid. p. 429; and in Plato, *Timaeus* 41B, ed. Waszink, p. 35. For detailed discussion, see Romig, pp. xxiv, xxxv, xlvii-xlviii; D.E. Luscombe, "Nature in the Thought of Peter Abelard," *La Filosofia della Natura nel Medioevo*, Atti del 3. Congreso Internazionale di Filosofia Medioevale (Milan, 1966), pp. 314-19; Tullio Gregory, "Abélard et Platon," *Peter Abelard*, ed. E.M. Buytaert (Louvain, 1971), pp. 60-63 and "Ratio et Natura ches Abélard," *Pierre Abélard-Pierre le Vénérable*, Colloques Internationaux du CNRS no. 546 (Paris, 1975), pp. 569-81).

[22] Dales, p. 182.

[23] See text in note 21 above.

[24] Hugh, *Tractatus* 11, 20, 30 (pp. 241, 249, 253).

[25] "In his uero quae condidit, causas naturales inseruit. Ex causis superioribus pendet rerum necessitas, ex causis inferioribus naturarum est possibilitas. Pro causis superioribus, necesse est fieri quod cumque sit; pro causis inferioribus, possibile est de rebus hoc fieri quod sit; . . . Vide ergo pro causa superiori, id est pro uoluntate Dei, quae libera semper existit, omnia necessario fieri. Sed quae facta sunt, quia de nichilo processerunt, mutabilitati obnoxia sunt. Pro causis igitur suae mutabilitatis efficitur ex eis, quod Deus prefixit in eis posse fieri ex eis, nec tamen necesse sit"; ed. Lacomte, ch. 14 (pp. 245-46), translation mine.

[26] See text in note 21 above.

[27] Hugh, *Tractatus* 19 (p. 248): "Naturarum igitur conditionem, legem et ordinem scias esse creatoris solummodo voluntatem."

[28] Abelard, *Expositio* (ed. Romig, p. 22).

[29] Hugh, *Tractatus* 6: "Inde per Moysen scriptum est: *Creauit Deus*. Pro hoc uoce quam dicimus Deus, in hebreo 'elohim' scribitur. Elohim uero apud Hebreos uox est pluralis, sed idioma linguae latinae hoc transferre non potuit. Sic est enim apud Hebreos, 'bara elohim,' ut si uerbum ex uerbo transferas, latino sermone contra morem oporteat dici 'creauit dii.' Unde sciendum est, quia uox illa elohim Deum significans enunciatione plurali, non tamen plures deos ponere potuit, quod determinat apud Hebreos uox adiecta singularis, id est 'bara,' quod est apud latinos 'creauit.' Hunc sermonem hebraicum catholici nostri recte sic positum pie defendunt, qui trinitatem quae Deus est in unitate simplici predicant adorari, quam representat eis uox singularis adiecta plurali, id est 'bara elohim.'" Compare this with Abelard, *Expositio in hexameron* (ed. Romig, p. 22): "Ubi autem nos dicimus: *Creavit deus*, pro eo quod est deus, in Hebreo habetur 'heloym,' quod divinarum personarum pluralitatem ostendit. 'Hel' quippe singulare est, quod interpretatur 'deus'; 'heloym' vero plurale est, per quod diversitatem personarum, quarum unaqueque deus est intelligimus. Provide autem dictum est: 'Heloym creavit,' non 'creaverunt,' ut videlicet ad plurale nomen singulare verbum referretur; quatinus insinuaretur in tribus illis personis non tres creatores, sed unum tantum debere intelligi. Cum igitur dixit 'Heloym creavit,' in quo divinas personas pariter cooperari docuit, profecto indivisa esse opera trinitatis prefixit. Cum autem postmodum, ut diximus, patris et spiritus et verbi personas distinxit, in quo illa consisteret trinitas determinavit." See also Isidore, *Etymologiae* 8.1.3, ed. W. M. Lindsay (Oxford, 1911); cited also in Abelard's *Theologia 'Summi boni'* 1.2, ed. H. Ostendler, *Beiträge zur Geschichte der Philosophie und der Theologie des Mittelalters* 35, part 2 (Münster i. W., 1939), p. 4-5; *Theologia Christiana* 1.8-9, ed. Eligius M. Buytaert, O.F.M., *Petri Abaelardi Opera Theologica* 2, Corpus Christianorum Continuatio Mediaeualis 12 (Turnholt, 1969), p. 75; *Theologia scholarium* (*tsch*) 76-77, ibid., p. 432; *Theologia Scholarium* 1.69-70 (PL 178:998).

[30] Leif Grane, *Peter Abelard: Philosophy and Christianity in the Middle Ages*, trans. Frederick and Christine Crowley (New York, 1970), p. 100.

[31] Hugh, *Tractatus* 38 (pp. 260-61): "Proponimus quia Deus fecit omnia bonus bona, et quia extra haec utique sunt nulla." Cf. Abelard, *Expositio* (ed. Romig, p. 84; PL 178:766); David E. Luscombe,*The School of Peter Abelard* (Cambridge, 1969), p. 292.

[32] A. Victor Murray, *Abelard and Bernard* (Manchester, 1967), p. 24; Grane, p. 125.

[33] Luscombe, p. 178.

[34] See the extensive discussion of this, and pertinent bibliography, in Romig, pp. xli-xlvii.

[35] Hugh, *Tractatus* 8 (p. 242); see also *Capitula haeresum Petri Abaelardi* 1, ed. Buytaert, *Petri Abaelardi Opera Theologica* 2, Corpus Christianorum Continuatio Mediaeualis 12 (Turnholt, 1969), p. 473.

[36] Hugh of St. Victor, *De sacramentis Christianae fidei* 1.2.22 (PL 175:38-41).

[37] Hugh, Tractatus 35 (pp. 259-60).

[38] Abelard, *Expositio* (ed. Romig, pp. 72-73); Mary M. McLaughlin, "Peter Abelard and the Diginity of Women: Twelfth Century 'Feminism' in Theory and Practice," *Pierre Abélard--Pierre le Vénérable* (Paris, 1975), pp. 295, 305-6, 325.

[39] Otto of Freising, *The Deeds of Frederick Barbarossa* 1.54, trans. C. C. Mierow (New York, 1953).

A Thirteenth-Century Teaching Aid: An Edition of the Bodleian *Abbreviatio* of the Pseudo-Aristotelian *De plantis*

R. James Long

Contained in two Bodleian Library manuscripts, Tanner 116 (fols. 88r-90r) and Digby 17 (fols. 166r-171r), is a commentary on the pseudo-Aristotelian treatise entitled *De plantis* or *De vegetabilibus*. On paleographic grounds Daniel Callus dates the production of the former version to the middle of the thirteenth century and the latter to the late thirteenth or early fourteenth century.[1] The author, once wrongly thought to have been the Oxford master Simon of Faversham,[2] has yet to be identified.[3] In form the work is an epitome or *abbreviatio*, with nearly a third of the text consisting of quotations or close paraphrases of the *De plantis* and with the overall length totaling approximately 44% of the same work. Though he does not mention Alfred of Sareshel (or Alveredus Anglicus) by name, two verbatim citations testify to the Bodleian master's acquaintance with Alfred's *Glossae*, the first such commentary by a Latin author.[4]

The Bodleian *abbreviatio* is clearly a product of the schools, and more particularly of the exigencies of the Arts curriculum, the necessity, namely, of covering a set text in a limited period of time. In fact, if the statutes of the University of Paris be any guide to the practice at Oxford, the time assigned to the philosophy of plants was a brief five weeks.[5] In other words, the *abbreviatio* edited below is one master's attempt to abridge the material of the *De plantis*, recasting it at the same time in a more easily assimilable form.[6] Although the author exhibits a marked propensity for numbered lists -- seven reasons why plants are not superior to animals, five material principles of plants, seven causes of the special properties of plants, and so forth -- there is no serious attempt to restructure the work nor to relate it to the rest of the Aristotelian corpus: indeed the author cites only the *Metheora*.

The anonymous Bodleian *abbreviatio*, in short, belongs to the genre of teaching aids -- a kind of condensation of material which was probably as much in demand among students in the thirteenth century as today. Precisely as aids to learning, such epitomes played a distinct, even though minor, role in the scholastic process of assimilating the natural philosophy of Aristotle, including the philosophy of plants.[7]

The Edition

In preparing an edition of the Bodleian *abbreviatio,* use was made of the following *sigla*:

D = Oxford, Bodleian Library, MS Digby 17, fols. 166r-71r.
T = Oxford, Bodleian Library, MS Tanner 116, fols. 88r-90r.

In cases where divergent readings were both grammatically and doctrinally correct, the tendency was to favor the reading of the Tanner text, simply because it was earlier; notwithstanding, in a majority of cases *D*'s readings were clearly preferable. Though the two versions are fairly closely related, *D* could not have been copied from *T* or any of *T*'s direct descendants. It is rather the case that both issued ultimately from a common source, with the scribe of *T* exhibiting a carelessness that is generally absent from the more recent *D*.

The *lemmata,* which are written in bold script in both *D* and *T*, have been reproduced in capitals. The direct citations and close paraphrases of the text of the *De plantis* have been indicated by italicizing, without however giving the locations in the recent edition by Drossaart Lulofs.[8] The two direct citations from Alfred's glosses are included in quotation marks.

The orthography of the edition follows that of the manuscripts as closely as possible. Punctuation, capitalization, and paragraph divisions conform to the canons of modern English. Letters and words supplied by the editor are enclosed in caret brackets (< >).

The support of the Research Committee of Fairfield University, which enabled the purchase of the microfilms, is acknowledged with gratitude.

Notes

[1] Though Callus does not assert that the latter manuscript was copied from the former, both scribes give the treatises, which collectively comprised the *Corpus Vetustius*, in the same order ("Introduction of Aristotelian Learning to Oxford," *Proceedings of the British Academy* 29 [1943], 50).

[2] A. Hackman (*Catalogi Codicum Manuscriptorum Bibliothecae Bodleianae, Pars Quarta* [Tanner MSS], [Oxford, 1860], p. 494) based his attribution to Simon of Faversham on the authority of a table of contents in a fly leaf of Tanner MS 116; S. D. Wingate accepted uncritically Hackman's attribution (*The Mediaeval Latin Versions of the Aristotelian Scientific Corpus, with Special Reference to the Biological Works* [London, 1931], pp. 68-69).

[3] Callus rejected the evidence advanced by Hackman as ambiguous and too late to be of value; internal evidence, moreover, reveals that the *abbreviationes* in the Tanner and Digby manuscripts bear less resemblance to the authenticated works of Simon of Faversham than to the technique of

Grosseteste's *summa abbreviata* on the *Ethics* ("Aristotelian Learning," p. 51). Cf. C. H. Lohr, "Medieval Latin Aristotle Commentaries," *Traditio* 29 (1973), 146.

[4] See my edition of Alfred's commentary in *Mediaeval Studies* 47 (1985), 125-67. The Bodleian master's use of this commentary not only points to a post-1210 composition date (see ibid., p. 130) but also provides, together with its provenance, an argument that the Bodleian master was an Oxonian; no Parisian master, with the exception of Peter of Auvergne, is known to have cited Alfred's glosses.

[5] See the statute of the faculty of Arts dated 19 March 1255 (*Chartularium Universitatis Parisiensis*, ed. H. Denifle and A. Chatelain [Paris, 1889], 1:278). Although the first Oxford statute governing the Arts curriculum, dated 1268, does not specifically prescribe lectures on the *De plantis*, there was a provision for the substitution at the discretion of the masters of a book other than the one assigned (*Statuta Antiqua Universitatis Oxoniensis*, ed. S. Gibson [Oxford, 1931], pp. 25-27). In fact, the *De plantis* is not explicitly mentioned as part of the Arts curriculum until a statute of 1431 (ibid., pp. 234-35). In the absence of evidence to the contrary, however, one may presume that the *mos Parisiensis* was observed for the most part at Oxford as well.

[6] The work is made up of some 107 generally brief paragraphs, most introduced by the conjunction *item*.

[7] See Callus, pp. 49, 52-53.

[8] See full citation in the apparatus to the text.

<Abbreviatio librorum De plantis>

<I>

<V>ITA IN ANIMALIBUS ET PLANTIS INUENTA EST per multos effectus, IN ANIMALIBUS MANIFESTA APPARENS, IN PLANTIS UERO OCCULTA, NON EUIDENS, et cetera. Capituli primi. Et primo ponit sententiam opinantium plantas esse animalia quedam, ut Anaxagore dicentis eas tristari, cuius signum est quod florum et fructuum et frondium habundantiam tanquam molestantia abiciunt; Abrucallus autem posuit ibi sexum esse. Plato uero posuit in eis desiderium *propter uehementem*

3 per . . . cetera *om. T* **6** sententiam] sententias *D* **8** Abrucallus] Arbugales *D*; autem] *om. D*; **9** sexum] sextum *T*

5 Nicolaus Damascenus, *De plantis*, ed. H. J. Drossaart Lulofs and E. L. J. Poortman, in *Nicolaus Damascenus, De plantis. Five Translations, Aristoteles Semitico-Latinus* (Amsterdam, Oxford, New York, 1989), p. 517

nutrimenti necessitatem, uocans "uim attractatiuam et retentatiuam et digestiuam desiderium."

Item *quidam dicunt plantas habere animam, quia generari, nutriri, augeri, in iuuentute uirescere, senioque dissolui* perceperunt in eis et cum hiis *desiderio affici;* et cum hec sint communia animalibus, etiam posuerunt eas esse animalia.

Item *quicquid cibatur, desiderat et delectatur saturitate, tristaturque, cum esurit.* Sed hec non fiunt sine sensu. Sed plante nec sensum nec desiderium neque organa senciendi neque etiam signum aliquod sensum habent. Ergo, et cetera. Vnde quod planta sit animata solum per nutrimentum et augmentum, que sunt effectus partium anime, confirmat et sic destruit opiniones aliorum.

Item *sensus est causa illustrationis uite, nutrimentum uero causa augmenti rei uiue,* quia "uita sine sensu mortis tenet ymaginem."

Item cum in plantis non sit uera nec perfecta uita, scilicet illustrata, nec omnino priuatio uite, cum sint ibi partes uite, nec potest inter animatum et inanimatum poni medium, patet quod diminute respectu animalium dicuntur habere uitam et esse animata. Plante itaque priuate sensu non sunt dicenda animalia, *quia genera dant suis speciebus nomina et diffinitiones et similiter species suis indiuiduis.*

Item *sunt animalia que sexu carent femineo et que non generant* ut musce; *sunt etiam que non mouentur; sunt etiam que prolem sibi dissimilem producunt.*

Item *sensus facit discretionem in mortem et uitam; sed celum, quia habet regnum nobilius et dignius nostro regimine, elongatum est ab hiis. Oportet autem, ut animal perfectum et diminutum habeant commune aliquod, et hec est inuentio uite.*

Item planta non caret anima, *quia in ea est aliqua pars anime; et non est animal, quia in ea non est sensus.*

Item singula corruptibilia *exeunt de uita ad non uitam paulatim.*

Item *habet membra determinata. Sed planta indeterminata.*

Item *attrahere cibum ex principio naturali est commune animali et plante* et *non erit nisi cum attractione cibi sensus omnino* (verior littera sine "nisi").

Item *omne cibabile utitur in sua cibatione duabus rebus scilicet calore et*

14 sint] sicut *T*; eas] *om. T* **16** tristaturque] tristatur quia *T* **18** organa] organum *D* **19** solum] scilicet *D* **20** confirmat] constat *D*; destruit] destruxit *D* **23** ymaginem] ymaginationem *T* **24** nec[1]] et D **29** species] *om. T* **30** carent] carut (*sic*) *T*; femineo] feminino *T*; ut musce *om. T* **31** mouentur] mouetur *T* **35** habeant] habeat *D*

10 R. James Long, "Alfred of Sareshel's Commentary on the Pseudo-Aristotelian *De plantis*," *Mediaeval Studies* 47 (1985), 147 **23** Ibid., p. 151 **42** The Drossaart Lulofs edition in fact omits *nisi* (p. 521)

frigore, et eget anima cibo humido et cibo sicco, quia frigiditas est in humido cibo, caliditas *uero in sicco, quia nulla istarum duarum naturaliter separatur a socio suo.*

PERSCRUTEMUR ID QUOD PRECESSIT ET CETERA. Ca. secundum. Nota quod *inuenimus multa animalia* non habencia spiramen et *quod plante nisi dormiunt neque uigilant, quia uigilare est ex effectu sensus et dormire est debilitas sensus,* quorum nihil est in re uegetabili cum careat sensu.

Item *quando cibatur animal, ascendit uapor a cibo eius usque ad capud et dormit; et quando* consumitur *uapor ille, multus que tamen parum dormiunt. Et dormitio motus compressio, et compressio est quies rei mote.*

Postea de sexu in plantis nota: *masculinus quando generat, in aliud generat, et femininum quando generat, ab alio generat, et sunt ambo separata a se; et illud non inuenitur in plantis, quia quelibet species plante mascule est asperior et durior et rigidior, et femina debilior et fructifera.*

Item Arburgales posuit istas species in plantis esse commixtas quod inprobat per hoc principium: quecumque commixta sunt, prius fuerunt simplicia in se, et ita *erit per se masculus et per se femina.*

Item si sic esset -- et tunc unum et idem simul et respectu eiusdem -- esset agens et paciens et etiam *planta esset perfectior animali, quia non indigeret in sua generatione re extrinseca* -- quod patet falsum. *Indiget enim temporibus anni et sole et temperantia anni et vere plus omni re. Et hoc in hora pululationis arborum.*

Item terra est principium generationis plantarum et sol fructuum et *terra mater plantarum et sol pater.* Postea dicit quod aliter ymaginanda est mixtio masculi et femine in animalibus et aliter in plantis, *quia semen plante simile est impregnationi, que est mixtio masculi et femine* animalium. *Et sicut est in ouo vis generandi pullum et materia cibi ipsius pulli gignendi usque ad horam exitus* ab ouo quod gallina ponit, ita et planta segregat humorem seminarium et eius nutrimentum simul; et hoc ultimum exitum confirmat auctoritate Arburgalis, dicentis quod *arbores alte non generant pullos,* id est ramos et surculos. Sed potius in radice *nascens* ex humore seminario *mouet se statim* sursum ramus genitus. Sic ergo conuenit plantarum generatio cum generatione quorumdam animalium; differt tamen in hoc quod planta plante numquam commiscetur in coitu sicut animalia. Postea ponit errorem opinantium plantam esse perfectiorem animali uel adeo perfectam, tum quia habet utrumque sexum, tum qua cibatur continue, tum quia tantum durat, tum quia in ea non est superfluum. Sed intellige: duplex est superfluitas in

45 cibo] cibus *D*; caliditas] calidita (*sic*) *D* **49** est[2]] *om. D* **52** consumitur] sumitur *D* **56** quelibet species: quedam sunt *T* **57** et durior *bis T* **59** commixta] mixta *D* **61** et tunc . . . planta *om. T* **70** pullum] pulli *T* **71** et] est *D* **72** eius] *om. T*

47 Drossaart Lulofs, p. 521

animali: una scilicet humoris nutritiui superflui, hic est humor seminarius -- et hec est necessaria uel utilis que est reperitur in plantis; alia est sicut urine et egestiones que emittuntur -- et hec non est necessaria et non est in planta. Deinde destruit hunc errorem 7 rationibus, ostendens animal esse perfectius planta, tum quia planta non mouetur motu processiuo, cum sit fixa in terra; vnde non indiget sompno propter fatigationem nec uoluntario; vnde nec sensum nec perfectam animam habet; tum quia planta alia est propter animal et non econtrario; tum quia planta continuo et uili et malo indiget cibo; tum quia tunc esset inanimatum dignius animato; tum quia opus animalis nobilius est, scilicet cognitio sensibilis, quam plante; tum quia in animali est omnis uirtus que est in planta et multe alie; tum quia animal generatur sub completiori esse quam planta, et supponit hec ratio rerum productionem inesse in mundi exordio fuisse successiuam, ut dicitur in Genesi, cui tamen ipse obuiat sic: *mundus totalis est perpetuus sempiternus, nec cessauit numquam generare animalia et plantas et omnes suas species.*

ET IN QUALIBET SPECIE PLANTARUM EST CALOR ET HUMOR NATURALIS QUE QUANDO CONSUMMABITUR INFIRMABITUR ET VETERASCET ET AREFIET ET CORRUMPETUR et cetera. Cap. 3, in quo principaliter de simplicibus partibus plantarum instituit sermonem; quibusdam tamen interpositis. Nota: quedam arbores habent humorem, et quia humor non est pars manifesta, ponit pro eo humores, distillantes ab errore extra, ut *gummi, resinam, mirram, thus, et gummi arabicum.*

Item partes plantarum multipliciter diuidit innuendo et est summa: partes uel sunt simplices uel composite. Simplices uel que nutriunt uel que nutriuntur, et hee uel sunt interius uel exterius; interius uel in qua digeritur nutrimentum, scilicet humor uel uenter, uel per quam defertur, ut vena, uel pars coniungens singula membra, ut nodus, uel que coniungitur, ut lignum, uel que generatur in partibus fornis, ut medulla; exterius, ut cortex, folia; partes que nutriunt, ut humores; partes composite, ut rami, uirge.

Item sicut sunt in animali membra similium partium, ut caro et os, et dissimilium, ut ramus, radix, et huiusmodi. Similiter in plantis. Vnde cortex plante comparatur cuti animalis; radix ori; nodi neruis.

Item lutum dupliciter diuiditur: uno modo per terram et aquam; alio modo per partes continuas, ut terram et terram. Primo modo in partes dissimiles; secundo in similes.

Item *fructuum quidam sunt compositi ex paucis, ut poma; quidam ex multis, ut fructus oliue qui habent corticum, carnem,* scilicet quod est comestibile

83 et[2]] que D **88** tum[1]] *om. D* **92** esse] *om. D*; rerum] non *T* **93** Genesi] genui *T* **96** est calor: et color *T*; et humor . . . corrumpetur *om. T* **105** hee] hec *T* **108** fornis] for (*sic*) *D* **110** ut] et *T* **114** in] per *D* **115** similes] consimiles *D* **116** quidam[1]] *bis T*

93 Gen. 1-2.2 **98** Drossaart Lulofs, p. 525

in ipso fructu, *et testam et semen. Quidam habent tres cooperaturas*, ut maiores nuces.

Item quamuis plante comparentur animalibus quo ad partes eorum, non tamen sunt similes quo ad operationes partium et effectus eorum.

Item quedam florum fructuum et foliorum durant per totum annum, que scilicet generantur ab humore unctuoso; quedam uero non, in quibus scilicet humor vitalis cito euaporatur a calore exteriori. Similiter est in omnibus fructibus cadentibus.

Item quamuis flores et fructus sunt partes plantarum, tamen partes ille decidunt toto permanente, et hoc quia sunt partes non determinate, sicut capilli et pili et ungues et cornua cerui.

Item differunt plante *in multitudine et paucitate;* et *in magnitudine et paruitate; in fortitudine et debilitate;* partes enim rariores debiliores sunt; *et hoc quia humor, qui est in magnis arboribus, in quibusdam est ut lac, ut in ficubus, et in quibusdam similes est pici, ut in vite, et in quibusdam est originalis, ut que est in origano*, ut inopigalium uel salum.

DIUERSITAS AUTEM PLANTE IN SUIS PARTIBUS COGNITA EST, et cetera. 4 cap., in quo de partibus plantarum dissimilibus siue compositis sermonem instituit. Nota: *quedam plantarum producunt fructum super folia sua*, ut que habent humorem seminarium ualde subtilem, *quedam sub foliis*, ut habentes minus subtilem, *quarumdam uero fructus suspensus est a stipite*, ut habentes grossum, et *quarumdam a radice, ut arbores Egypti, que dicuntur margaritio*, et *quarumdam fructus in medio earum*, ut habentes humorem seminarium mediocrem.

Item *radix plante mediatrix est inter plantem et cibum, et ideo vocant eam Greci principium et causam vite plantarum, quia ipsa causa vite* adducit. *Sed stipes plante est que sola nascitur a terra et est similis stature arboris; surculi uero que a radice arboris pululant rami que crescunt supra surculos*.

Item quedam plante, ut fungi et tuberes, non habent ramos nec folia.

Item *cortices et lignum et medulla arboris nascuntur a* superfluitate humoris, et quidam vocant hanc medullam *arboris matricem, quidam uero arboris* uiscera, *quidam uero cor. Et nodi et uene et caro totius plante ex 4 elementis sunt*. Similiter et fructus et rami et cortex.

PLANTARUM QUEDAM SUNT ARBORES ET CETERA. 5 cap., in quo diuidit per duas specificas plantas, conuenienter addens diuersitates que insunt

121 sunt] *om. T* **123** scilicet[2]] est *add. D* **129** et[2]] *om. D* **131** in ficubus: inferioribus *T* **133** origano] organo *T*; ut[2]] et *T*; uel salum *om. T* **134** et cetera *om. T* **137** subtilem] subtile *D* **138** quarumdam] quorumdam *D* **139** quarumdam] quorumdam *D* **140** quarumdam] quorumdam *T* **141** mediocrem: medio tantum *T* **143** adducit] adiuit *T* **145** surculos] circulos *T* **149** uiscera] uicera *T*

135 Ibid., p. 528 **151** Ibid., p. 530

eis a locis sue generationis; postea diuersitates que insunt eis secundum fructus et cooperimenta addit. Diuidit ergo plantam in 4 sic: plantarum alia est completa quoad habitum partium integralium prenominatarum et dicitur arbor; quedam uero incompleta que solum habet vnam permanentem, ut radicem, et aliam non permanentem, ut folia, et hec proprie dicitur herba; quedam autem media inter hec que subdiuiditur. Aut enim se habet per eque distantiam ad extrema, scilicet per medium, ut quod habet stipitem et folia et flores, et dicitur *olus regium;* aut quod magis conuenit cum proximo suo primo extremo, ut que habet stipitem et ramos et radices et dicitur olus; aut magis conuenit ad secundum extremum, ut que habet radices et ramos et folia sed non stipitem, et dicitur frutex, et sumit huius duas per effectus propter latenciam duarum specificarum.

Item quedam natuntur tamquam plante siue herbe et postea fiunt arbores.

Item *quedam plante sunt domestice, quedam ortenses, quedam siluestres, similiter et animalia.* Et omnes plante quando non fuerint culte siluestrescunt.

Item *arbores siluestres magis fructificant quam ortenses, sed fructus ortensium meliores sunt quam siluestrium.*

Item quedam plante nascuntur in locis siccis, ut oliua et ficus, et etiam in tectis et in uenis silicum quod contingit de semine granorum et reliquarum auium et tales oportet stercorare, aliter non durant; quedam in maribus quorum natura grossa est terrea et aquea; quedam uero in aliis fluminibus quorum natura subtilior; quedam in mari rubeo, ubi dominatur caliditas et humiditas, et ideo illic sunt magne quedam in ripis fluminum; quedam in stagnis.

Item *planta multum permutatur propter diuersitatem locorum.*

Item quidam loci fertiliores sunt aliis. Similiter quidam loci meliores fructus reddunt aliis locis.

Item *quarumdam plantarum sunt folia aspera, quarumdam leuia, quarumdam scissa, ut vitis.*

Item *quedam habent unum corticem, ut ficus, quedam* habent *multos, ut pinei, quedam uero sunt tote cortex medianus.*

Item *squilla unam tantum habet radicem et unum solum ramum emittit proceditque inferius dilatando se, quandoque magis creuerit, et calor solis ad ipsam accesserit, augebitur,* et est herba marina amarissima et extinguit venenum.

Item *succorum fructuum quidam sunt potabiles, ut succus vuarum, malorum* granatorum *et mororum; quidam impotabiles, ut succus oliue et*

153 eis[1]] ipsis *D*; insunt] sunt *D* **156** uero] autem *D* **159** per] *om. T*; quod] que *D* **160** quod] que *D*; proximo suo *om. T* **162** et[1]] *om. D* **168** siluestrescunt] siluestresint *T* **172** silicum] similiter *T* **174** uero] *om. D* **176** illic] illius *T* **181** quarumdam[2]] quorumdam *T* **182** quarumdam] quorumdam *T* **183** Item] et *T*; habent[2]] *om. T* **185** squilla] squilia *T* **190** granatorum] granorum *T*

nucis, quia sunt vnctuosi; quidam dulces, ut dactili et ficus; quidam calidi et acuti, ut origani et synapis; quidam amari, ut absinthium. Similiter fructuum, quidam compositi sunt ex carne, osse, et grano, ut pruna; quidam ex carne et grano, ut cucumeres; quidam ex humore et grano, ut mala granata.

Item *quidam fructus cito* maturantur, *ut mora et cerasa; quidam tarde, ut omnes fructus siluestres, ut plures eorum; et quedam plante cito producunt folia et fructus et eorum qui non maturescunt ante hyemem* et hec propter humorem terrestrem et aquosum habundantem.

Item *arborum aromaticarum quarumdam radix aromatica est, quarumdam cortex, quarumdam flos, quarumdam lignum, quarumdam uero omnes partes, ut balsamus.*

ET QUEDAM ARBORES NASCUNTUR PLANTATE. 6 cap., in quo de diuersitate dispositionum plantarum secundum propagationem per quam continuatur successio et specei conseruatio et de dispositionibus earum ad fecunditatem et sterilitatem et de transmutatione earum ad speciem a specie. Dicit ergo quod *quedam plante nascuntur per plantationem; quedam per seminationem; quedam per se,* scilicet ex commixtione caloris et sicci cum humido terreo. *Eorum uero que per plantationem uel a radice euelluntur uel a stipite uel a ramis uel a semine uel tota planta transfertur a loco, ut alibi plantetur; quedam uero parum contuse. Similiter quedam plantantur in terra; quedam arboribus sunt insite et melior est insitio similium in similia conproportionalia. Talia enim optime proueniunt, ut mali in pirum, et quandoque fit insitio in diuersis generibus,* quandoque in eodem, ut fici in ficum.

Item *a quibus malis seminibus bone arbores proueniunt, ut ab amigdalis amaris* dulcia.

Item *non prouenit de facili ex semine,* id est fructu, *malo planta bona nec ex fructu bono arbor mala.* Sed *in animali pluries sic accidit. Arbor quoque durum habens corticem, sterilis effecta, si findatur radix eius, et fissure illi lapis immitatur, rursus fiet fecunda; si etiam folia uel puluis foliorum uel cortex palme* mascule *apponantur ad palmam feminam uento agitate, cito maturabuntur fructus eius prohibuntque casum eorum. Similiter ficus siluestres expanse super radicem ficus ortensis conferunt eis maturitatem.*

191 nucis] nitis *T* **195** maturantur] marterantur *T*; cerasa] *om. T* **200** uero] *om. T* **202** plantate *ed.*: plante *DT*; et cetera *add. D* **204** successio] successiuo *T*; conseruatio] continuatio *T* **207** commixtione] mixtione *T* **208** Eorum] earum *T* **210** contuse] confuse *T* **212** conproportionalia] proportionalia *T* **215** quibus] quibusdam *T* **217** prouenit] proueniunt *T*; de facili ex semine: ex facili de semine *D*; planta bona: plante bone *T* **218** arbor mala: arbores male *T*; Sed] licet *T*; pluries] plures *T*; accidit] accidat *T* **219** fissure] fissurs (*sic*) *T* **220** si] sicut *T* **221** mascule] macule *T*; uento agitate *om. T*

202 Ibid., p. 534

Item palma mascula discernitur a femina, quia mascula prius pululat et folia eius minora et odor maior est. Nota: dicit Flotimus quod palma crescit directe surgens a terra, et simul a principio ortus sui habet formam omnium partium completam; sed non incompleta magnitudine, sicut spica incassa. Si etiam fuerint multe palme femine circumstantes unam masculam, omnes ex ipsa concipient et in tempore pullulationis et conceptionis stabit mascula hirsuta, foliis et ramis expansa vndique uelud uir; femina autem stabit inclinans ramos suos ad masculam et tamquam compta habens folia et ramos equaliter se habentia, et si uentus eo tempore, fugauerit odorem et calorem mascule. A quibusdam feminis in una parte stantibus ille non concipient in anno illo, sed tantum alie, ad quas peruenit calor et odor. Et postea ramos suos erigunt quod prius inclinabant. Insuper si excidatur mascula, fiunt infecunde omnes femine que ab ipsa concipere solent et sterilescunt.

Item quedam plante transmutantur in aliam speciem, ut nux cum inueterata fuerit; similiter *triticum et linum perniciosum nascitur in Persia et transplantatum in Egyptum et Ierusalem factum est commestibile. Similiter amigdala et mala granata mutantur a sua malicia per culturam. Similiter mala granata stercore porcino fimata, et aqua frigida dulci rigata, melioratur.* Similiter et *plante siluestres hoc artificio* per scissionem radicum et fimationem *fiunt ortenses. Locus uero et labor huic rei conferunt et maxime tempore anni in quo plantantur.*

Item *uer multum congruit plantationi hyemps et autumpnus, parum estas uero, minime post ortum stelle canicule.*

Item *in Egypto non fit plantatio, nisi semel in anno.*

Item *quedam arbores ex suis radicibus producunt folia* et cetera.

Item arbores que pluries in anno fructificant earum ultimi fructus frequenter remanent crudi et immaturi propter frigiditatem hyemis superuenientis.

Item quedam diu uacant a fructu, ut ficus.

Item *quedam vno fructificant anno et alio reficiuntur* solem attrahendo humorem ad nutrimentum, *ramos tamen multos producunt; quedam in iuuentute sterliores sunt quam in senectute; quedam econtrario, ut amigdali, piri, ylex.*

Item *masculus spissior est et solidior, durior, ramosior, minus humorosus, fluctus minor quantitate, minus maturabilis, folia diuersa, similiter et surculi.*

224 pululat] puluat *T* **230** foliis] *om. T* **236** omnes] *om. T* **237** inueterata] inueterat *D*

225 I have been unable to identify this authority.

<II>

PLANTA TRES HABET UIRES, PRIMAM EX GENERE TERRE, SECUNDAM EX GENERE AQUE, TERCIAM EX GENERE IGNIS ET CETERA.

A terra enim est fixio, siue immobilitas, eius; ab aqua coagulatio; ab igne partium coadunatio. Exemplificat de hiis tribus *in fictilibus*. Similiter est in omni animali et minera.

Item *in quo raritas non est, ita solidum est quod augeri non potest. Vnde lapides et terra et huiusmodi non augentur.*

Item plante uelocior est generatio quam animalis, quia magis assimulant quam animal et propter diuersitatem partium animalis. Vbi enim est diuersitas, oportet quod natura diucius laboret ad constitutionem huius. Et quia planta subtilius quid est quam animal. Vnde propter maiorem conformitatem caloris subtilis digerentis ad subtile quod digeritur, cicius generatur quod subtilius est: quod patet de planta per eius maiorem raritatem quam sit in animali. Vnde calor exterior uel interior *humorem ad extremitates plante trahit, et digeritur materia humorosa per omnes partes eius, et quod superfuerit,* emanabit ad generandum folia et flores et gummi, *sicut in balneo calor humorem* a fundo ad superficiem *attrahit* subtiliando ipsum, *et in vaporem conuertit quod eleuato,* cum multus fuerit et multum comprimitur, *uertitur in guttas.* Similiter in planta et animali humores superflui ascendunt ab inferioribus ad superiora et descendunt econtrario.

Item *quando ex pluuia multiplicantur aque* concauitate montium intercepte et tandem *interius constricte, fiet ex eis vapor magnus propter soliditatem terre scinditque terram* et apparebunt fontes.

Item *terre motus sepe ostendunt fontes in flumina, que prius non apparuere, quando scinditur terra ex vapore* agitato in ventre terre. *Sepe et fontes submerguntur per terre motum. Sed huiusmodi scissio non conuenit plantis propter raritatem partium* eius nec etiam in locis non solidis, ut in arenosis. Similiter fit terre motus ex aere calido et sicco incluso in concauitate terre et naturaliter ascendente et impetuose exeunte, *quia propter terre soliditatem non potest paulatim exire.*

Item aurum in aquam proiectum mergitur, et hoc propter soliditatem, non propter ponderositatem. Lignum uero supernatat non propter folia sed propter raritatem; similiter hebenus mergitur propter eius soliditatem.

13 propter] ponit *T* **14** cicius] ocius *T* **18** superfuerit] superfluit *T* **29** eius] *om. T* **34** uero] *om. D* **35** hebenus] ebanus *T*

3 Drossaart Lulofs, p. 539

Item *oleum et folia aque supernatant, quia in hiis est humor vnctuosus, cuius est consuetudo partibus coherere; est etiam calor arens qui facit ascendere illud quod ipsum consequitur ad partes aeris; aquam et rem habentem multum aeris facit ascendere ad superficiem eius.*

Item *quidam lapides supernatant propter inanitatem siue aeream vacuitatem multam in suis partibus.*

Item nota: natura aque est super terram ascendere; aeris uero super aquam. Vnde *lapis qui multum habet de terrestritate, mergitur in aqua; habens uero multum aeris inclusi, ascendit super aquam; qui autem mediocriter mixtus, medietas eius mergitur et medietas supernatat.* Quodlibet enim suum simile attrahit; si autem inequaliter sit mixtus, efficatior erit altera pars.

Item *ex collisione forti undarum maris arene congregat arena spumam vnctuosam, deinde coagulatur; tandem siccabitur per salsedinem* maris mixtam cum terrestritate et caliditate superfusa et sic spuma cum arena fit lapis.

Item *omnes terre sunt dulces in gustu.*

Item terre sunt salse propter siccitatem propriam et calorem agentem et mixtionem terre cum aqua.

Item dicit vnde arena in locis prope mare et alias aquas.

Item in locis non coopertis et ab aquis multum distantibus, fiunt arene per hoc quod solis calor ibi perseuerat, et omnem humiditatem ibidem desiccat remanente arena uel puluere terre absque omni humiditate.

Item *radix omnium aquarum dulcis est.*

Item quod subtilius est et maxime supereminens terre in aquis, hec naturalis aqua est.

Item quod aqua dulcis sit subtilior quam aqua sales probat experimento: *inpletis enim duobus uasis hoc aque dulci, illo aqua salsa et posito eodem ouo in utraque; in salsa natabit et in dulci mergetur.* Vnde cum sunt simul, *aqua dulcis supereminet salse et a terra est remotior et hec est naturalis aqua,* et est etiam terre impermixta.

Item in mari mortuo non generantur animalia propter eius frigiditatem nec merguntur propter eius densitatem.

Item *sal generatur in lacunis sic: primo ex aqua dulci fit aqua salsa; deinde salsedo terre superans salsedinem aque,* coagulat et exsiccat aquam salsam in salem. In quo sale, licet aliquid fuerit inclusum de subtili aereo, tamen non est in ipso dulcedo sensibilis propter salsedinem terrestrem uincentem.

37 est] *om. D*; arens] aereus *D* **41** vacuitatem] natiuitatem *T* **42** nota] *om. D* **53** propriam] in proprietate *D* **60** quod] *om. T* **62** sit] habet *T* **64** et] *om. T* **66** et] *om. D* **67** Item] *om. D*; non] nec *D* **69** Item] in *D* **70** superans] superhabundans *T*

EODEM MODO HERBE ET SPECIES NON FIENT NISI PER COMPOSITIONEM ET CETERA. 2 cap., in quo dicit generationem plante simpliciter, dicens quod plante non fiunt per naturam simplicem sed per mixtionem elementarem. Sic vapores elementares mediante calore ascendunt ad locum mixtionis, ubi etiam descendit aer madidus, rorificans illum locum mixtione; ad quem etiam uenit uirtus celestis, et infusa ipsis miscibilibus commiscet ea et coagulat in plantam.

Item aqua necessaria huic mixtioni non est qualiscumque sed dulcis et non salsa, quia aqua dulcis ascendit propter sui subtilitatem et nata est esse supra aquam salsam; et quanto plus incorporatur ei de subtili aereo, tanto plus subtiliatur et magis ascendit; et quod aqua dulcior et subtilior magis ascendit ostendit per 4 effectus: primus, quod propterea sunt fontes dulciores in montibus et flumina sunt dulciora; secundus, quod propterea fleuma et sanguis ascendunt ad cerebrum, scilicet propter suam dulcedinem et subtilitatem; tertius, quod propter hoc dulce et subtile de cibo ascendit ad partes superiores, et grossum et salsum ad inferiores--grossissimum et salsissimum et non conferens emittatur per egestiones; quartus, quod propterea ascendunt omnes aque ascendentes; illud enim quod subtile est etiam in aqua salsa, per calorem eleuatur in vaporem; illud quod eleuatur, quia habundat in ipso multum de subtili aereo, ideo dulce est, ut in balneo salso patet. Cuius partibus cum incorporatur calor subtiliat eas et eleuat ex ipsis vaporem, qui amittens salsedinem ascendit sensibiliter usque ad cooperimentum balnei, et cum ibi multiplicatur, ingrossatur et descendit in guttas dulces.

Item in aqua salsa non multum generantur plante propter frigiditatem et siccitatem terrestrem ibi habundantem.

Item in locis habundantibus niue raro generantur plante propter nimiam sui distemperantiam; quandoque tamen generantur ibi plante sine foliis et floribus.

Item in locis salsis et siccis raro generantur plante. Sed in locis montuosis est dulcedo et ideo conueniens est generationi.

Item in locis calidis ubi habundat humor dulcis, optime proueniunt propter vehementem caloris solaris sufficientis ad digerendum naturam plantarum, scilicet humorem dulcem.

Item locus arenosus inutilis est ad generationem plante propter salsedinem habundantem et siccitatem terrestrem, et si quas producunt, erunt sicce et parue.

74 nisi . . . compositionem *om. T* **75** in quo: primo *D* **78** madidus] matidus *T* **82** quia] si *add. D* **86** sunt] *om. D* **92** in] per *D*; quod eleuatur: que eleuatum *D* **100** generantur] generatur *D* **102** montuosis] vnctuosis *T* **103** est] *om. T* **105** solaris] *bis D*

75 Ibid., p. 545

PLANTE AUTEM QUE SUPERFICIEM AQUE ET CETERA. 3 cap., in quo de modis generationis plantarum et etiam de proprietatibus consequentibus diuersitatem localem. Dicit ergo quod humido aqueo stante et non currente ascendit quidem uapor grossus usque ad superficiem aque in similitudinem nubis nec ascendit ultra propter sui grossiciem. Vnde adueniente calore solis digeritur in plantam. Sed est sine radice. Habet etiam tantummodo folia lata.

Item in loco humido terrestri et fumoso detinente putredines, includentes aerem virtute uentorum et pluuiarum, exeunt ille putredines et per calorem solis digeruntur in plantis, vbi sunt fungi et tuberes.

Item in locis calidis, ut supra, proximo et idem sit in locis frigidis; frigus enim reprimit calorem et detinet in profundo terre, qui ibidem detentus humiditatem ibidem existentem digerit et producit ex ea plantam.

Item a locis dulcibus, ut frequenter, non separantur aque, ubi aer inclusus coagulabitur cum aqua et per calorem digeretur in plantam que non expandit folia. Sed crescit in longum tantum, ut neufar.

Item ubi currunt aque calide, calor ille uapores frigidos sursum attrahit, quos coagulatos cum aere humido digerit calor ille in plantam: sed non fit hoc nisi per longum tempus propter calorem accidentalem qui non congruit generationi.

Item plante nascentes *in locis sulphureis ut multum non habent multa folia quia remote sunt a temperantia.*

Item in tertio et quarto climate habundant magis plante, scilicet comestibiles et magis fructificant, et hoc propter habundantem calorem ibi existentem et temperamentum, et maxime in locis calidis, lenibus et altis et frigidis, et maxime in vere, quia tunc temperatur frigus per calorem.

Item subtile existens sub aqua dulci plantam unctuosam producit, cuius fructus ualde comestibilis est.

Item plante nascentes super lapides solidos diuturnam habent generationem et parum ascendunt et indigent terra circumstante et aqua irrigante et aere conueniente.

Item plante prope orientem cicius generantur, prope uero occidentem tardius.

111 plantarum] plante *T*; etiam] *om. D* **112** humido] +habitudo+ *T* **117** detinente] descendente *T* **119** digeruntur] digeritur *T*; vbi] vt *D* **122** existentem] existendum *D* **123** separantur] separentur *T* **125** neufar] nenufar *ed.* **127** sed . . . generationi *om. T* **131** sed hoc non fit nisi per longum tempus propter calorem accidentalem qui non congruit generationi *add. T* **132** scilicet] *om. T* **138** plante] plantas *D* **139** terra] *om. D* **141** plante] planta *D*; generantur] generatur *D*

110 Ibid., p. 548

Item planta in qua habundat niuis uel humiditas aquea uel siccitas male nutritur et dicit causas; sunt aut 4 quibus indiget maxime planta et etiam animal: primum, semen terminatum, id est humor seminarius neque superfluus neque diminutus; secundum, locus conueniens; tertium, aqua moderata; quartum, aer consimilis, quorum quolibet deficiente uel diminuto uel non omnino uel non bene crescet et nutritetur.

Item species medicinales crescentes in montibus altis efficaciores et aptiores sunt medicine, *fructus enim earum durior est ad digerendum et minus nutriens*.

Item in locis a sole remotis parum producentur plante uel animalia et hoc propter defectum caloris parum operantis ibi. Postea docet qualiter generantur ex grosso humore in aquis stantibus herba que dicitur "planta stagnorum," que non differt in forma et figura, et postea dat generationem plurium plantarum huiusmodi.

HERBE AUTEM ET QUICQUID CRESCIT SUPER TERRAM ET CETERA. 4 cap., in quo enumerat diuersa principia materialia omnium plantarum. *Et sunt 5, scilicet semen, putredo,* et hec est materia debita et non ordinata a natura; *humor aque, insitio,* postea de causis proprietatum plantarum generatarum, dicens quod quedam producunt fructus ante folia; quedam post; quedam ambo simul. Primum fit ex habundantia vnctuositatis et sufficientia caloris ad digerendum; secundum ex habundantia humiditatis et pauca vnctuositate recte proportionata humiditati.

Item dixerunt quidam quod folia et fructus idem sunt nisi quod minor est digestio in foliis quam in fructibus et in parte improbit dicens quod natura intendit facere folia, ut sint ad cooperimentum et tutelam fructuum. In quibusdam tamen arboribus sunt quandoque folia sine fructu, ut oliue. In alio uero anno, cum vigoratur calor sufficiens ad digerendum, producunt fructum; deinde dicit vnde spine et quare habent piramidalem figuram, quia scilicet humor vnde sunt quanto plus distat a planta, tanto subtilior est. Deinde dicit vnde color viridis in exteriori parte ligni et albus in interiori; et similiter folia arborum sunt quasi medii coloris inter ipsas arbores et earum flores.

Item triplex est figura plante in crescendo: quedam enim magis crescunt sursum; quedam magis deorsum; quedam equaliter. Causa primi est humor subtilis per calorem fere totaliter raptus sursum in meatibus ipsius plante et compressus per aerem existentem infra illos meatus piramidatur, sicut ignis

143 niuis] nimis *T* **147** quolibet] quosque *D* **149** species] etiam *T* **150** enim earum: uero ea *D* **151** nutriens] nutritiuus *T* **152** producentur] producuntur *T* **154** ex grosso: egresso *T* **157** ET] et cetera *om. T* **159** debita] indebita *T* **165** idem sunt *om. D* **169** digerendum] digerandum *T* **172** color] calor *T* **178** compressus] comprehensus *T*

158 Ibid., p. 552

in materia accensus. Causa secundi est humor grossus cum angustia meatuum, et ita duplex est causa quare partim ascendit. Causa tertii est humor medius inter grossum et subtilem et meatus medii inter nimis amplos et nimis angustos.

Item in plantis duplex est digestio: prima in radice; secunda in medulla. Vt cum fuerit humor digestus diuiditur in singulas partes, nec est ibi tertia digestio, sicut in animali: in singulis membris est propter diuersitatem in natura et in complexione ipsorum membrorum ipsius animalis.

Item arbor semper crescit dum viuit; animal uero non. Similiter in animali *sua longitudo propinqua est sue latitudini*, sed in arbore non.

DIUERSITAS QUOQUE IN RAMIS PLANTE EST EX SUPERFLUA RARITATE ET CETERA. 5 cap., in quo de causis proprietatum magis specialium prima proprietas dicta est; secunda de quantitate et casu foliorum. Et est humor rarus et uelociter fluxibilis causat etiam pirimidationem in figura foliorum. Talis enim humor in principio multum fluit et tunc sunt lata folia; deinde artius fluit et tunc artantur folia et sic piramidat. Tandem uero frigore obturante meatus inferiori parte plante, cessat fluxus humorum et siccantur folia et cadunt. Causa autem eius quod est non cadere est humor apposito medio se habens, scilicet spissus, vnctuosus, uiscosus. Vnde frigore aliquantulum opturante meatus nondum cadunt sed glauca fiunt; tertia de fructificatione plantarum; talis planta habens calorem semel in anno fructificat; planta uero non habens sufficientem vna vice digerit vnam partem et producit fructum ex eo, et tunc quiescit ut resumat uigorem quo suscepto. Digerit aliam partem humoris et digerit et producit in fructus et pluries fructificat in anno.

Item que habent humorem interminabilem et incoagulabilem et indigestibilem vix fructificant in anno; quarta proprietas est calor in planta.

Item planta habens angustos meatus et ideo non recipientes multum de aere mergitur in aqua.

Item quinta proprietas de causa florum est humor subtilis qui prius digeritur in flores quam grossus humor in fructum; quedam uero arbores non habent flores propter asperitatem et grossiciem in partibus plante contrariam nature florum, qui sunt ex materia leui et subtili.

Sexta proprietas est de multo cremento plantarum. Vnde planta habens grossos cortices multum crescit.

180 partim] parum *T* **184** in] ad *D* **187** dum] vnde *T* **189** ex . . . raritate *om. T* **194** sic piramidat: pirramidantur *T* **195** obturante] obscurantes *T* **197** uiscosus] uiterosus (*?*) *D* **199** semel] simul *T* **201** fructum] fructus *T*; ut resumat: et resumit *T* **202** digerit et *om. T* **205** est calor: colorum *D* **206** non] *om. T* **208** de] tam *T* **209** fructum] fructu *T*; non] *om. D*

190 Ibid., p. 556

Septima de gummi qui prouenit ex calore multo et aqua vnctuosa multa habundantibus in medulla arboris, ubi per digestionem conuertitur aqua hec in humorem similem lacti que postea euaporata usque ad extremitates plante fit gummi.

Item tripliciter generatur gummi: quoddam distillando quam distillationem facit calor et cum attigerit ad aerem frigidum, coagulatur mediocriter tamen; quoddam uero numquam coagulatur, quod scilicet manet in loco temperato; quoddam uero coagulatur induriciem lapideam ex vehementi frigiditate quod fit in locis superflue calidis, et hoc per frigus adueniens, vt enim habetur in libro 4 *Metheorum*. Illa fortissime coagulata sunt quorum coagulatio incepit a calido et terminatur per frigus. Huiusmodi enim ut frequenter sunt insolubilia, ut ibidem dicitur.

Item quedam plante sunt in vna parte anni vnius coloris, scilicet viridis; in alia uero parte anni alterius, scilicet glauci, quorum etiam fructus et folia non corrumpuntur in hyeme.

FRUCTUS UERO ERIT AMARUS QUANDO ET CETERA. 6 cap., in quo de causis proprietatum quarumdam cognitarum in fructu per gustum, ut de sapore fructuum; dicit ergo quod quando calor naturalis non est sufficiens ad terminandum et digerendum complete humorem ipsius fructus, tunc est sapor amarus cuius signum quod fructus amarus positus in ignem dulcessit et hoc propter digestionem factam ibi a calore ignis; et similiter frigidum et siccum terrestrem impediunt digestionem, sicut humidum interminabilem. Et per hoc intellige quando fructus est dulcis, scilicet quando naturalis calor est sufficiens ad terminandum et digerendum ipsum humidum.

Item *arbores que nascuntur in aqua acetosa* contrahunt acetosum humorem, et naturaliter frigidum et siccum, qui cum coagulatur in fructum, fit acetosi saporis in principio; deinde cum ille humor ulterius digeritur et acetositas paulatim tollitur, fit sapor dulcis in fructu. Tandem uero cum humor ille ultra modum siccatur et consumitur per calorem ipsa dulcedo uertitur in amaritudinem propter superfluam desiccationem et adustionem ipsius humoris.

Item in locis temperatis plante producunt fructus suos ante dies uernales, et hoc propter calorem naturalem sufficientem ad digerendum et maturandum humorem qui est materia fructus. Et ideo non exspectat calorem exteriorem.

Item omnes plante quando primo plantantur habent amarum fructum aut accedentem ad amaritudinem.

Item fructus mirabolanorum in principio sunt dulces; postea uero pontici; in fine uero amari. Mirabolanorum species sunt 5 bonorum.

214 et] *om. T* **217** gummi] +g . . . i+ *T* **227** scilicet] ut *T* **229** quando . . . cetera *om. T* **239** et[1]] *om. T* **240** acetosi] aceto *T*

222 Aristotle, *Meteor.* 4.6 (383a14-32) **228** Drossaart Lulofs, p. 559

Alfred of Sareshel's Commentary on Avicenna's *De congelatione et conglutinatione lapidum*

James K. Otte

Alfred of Sareshel (Alfredus Anglicus) was one of the principal twelfth-century translators from Arabic to Latin. He was also the first Latin commentator on Aristotle since Boethius (d. 524). Moreover, his commentaries on Aristotelian works establish him as a significant link in the reception and the dissemination of Graeco-Arabic thought in the Latin West.[1]

Alfred translated two works from Arabic into Latin: the *De plantis* or *De vegetabilibus,* now attributed to Nicholas of Damascus (1st cent. B.C.),[2] and a section of Avicenna's (d.1027) *Kitâb al-Shifâ',* known as the *De congelatione et conglutinatione lapidum* or *De mineralibus.*[3] During Alfred's time, however, both of these works were attributed to Aristotle. In addition, Alfred wrote gloss-like commentaries on the *De plantis,*[4] on the *Metheora*[5] and, if an entry in the catalogue of the Beauvais Cathedral Library, compiled in 1664, can be trusted, he also commented on the *De mundo et celo,* the *De generatione et corruptione,* the *De anima,* the *De sompno et vigilia,* the *De morte et vita,* and the *De colore celi.*[6] Finally, Alfred was the author of a highly influential and widely read independent treatise on the heart, called the *De motu cordis.*[7]

Although Alfred's commentary on the *De generatione et corruptione* has not been discovered, it is referred to elsewhere,[8] and he also cites it in his commentary on the *Metheora.*[9] Also, it has been suggested that with the *De colore celi* the *Metheora* may be meant,[10] but the other titles in the Beauvais Catalogue remain unsubstantiated.

However, yet another *opusculum* by Alfred, a commentary on that segment of Avicenna's *Kitâb al-Shifâ'* known by its Latin title as the *De congelatione et conglutinatione lapidum,* or *De mineralibus,* was encountered by this author in the course of preparing an edition of Alfred's commentary on the *Metheora.*[11] The existence of such a commentary is nowhere mentioned and, although its content was cited by other writers and credited to Alfred, those writers, as well as Alfred himself, were unaware that not Aristotle, but Avicenna was the source of their expositions on the formation of rocks.

This study will explain how and why this confusion originated, discuss the nature and content of the commentary as far as legibility of the defective manuscript allows, and offer a transcription of the *lemmata* with, as far as that is possible, the incipits and explicits of Alfred's glosses.

The translations of the *De plantis* and the *De mineralibus* established Alfred as a translator of Aristotle among his contemporaries. Modern scholarship, however, has deprived him of the distinction of having translated a work written by "the master of those who know," for neither treatise is now recognized as Aristotelian. The *De plantis* is now attributed to Nicholas of Damascus,[12] and *De mineralibus* to Avicenna.

What circumstances caused Alfred to translate Avicenna's section of the *Kitâb al-Shifâ'* in the belief that he had before him a part of Aristotle's *Metheora*? None other than Aristotle himself initiated the confusion when at the conclusion of the third book of the *Metheora* he promised a treatise dealing specifically with minerals.[13] So, when Alfred, working in Spain, discovered three anonymous chapters in Arabic dealing with the formation of mountains, stones, and minerals, he undoubtedly translated those into Latin and appended them to the *Metheora* translation in the belief that they were Aristotle's. The four books of the *Metheora* were translated separately from Greek and Arabic by Henry Aristippus (d. 1162) and Gerard of Cremona (d. 1187), to which Alfred added his translation of the three chapters, as this frequently found colophon indicates:

> Completus est liber metheorum cuius tres primus libros transtulit magister Gerardus Lumbardus summus philosophus de arabico in latinum. Quartum autem transtulit Henricus Aristippus de greco in latinum. Tria ultima capitula transtulit Aluredus Anglicus Sarelensis de arabico in latinum.[14]

But the "tria ultima capitula" proved to be not part of the *Metheora,* nor any other work of Aristotle, but rather a treatise on the formation of mountains, stones, and minerals by Avicenna.[15] What is even more significant, because of the dual authorship of the *Metheora,* i.e., with the discovery of Avicenna as the author of the "three last chapters," Alfred has become the translator of a separate treatise. Moreover, since his commentary on the *Metheora* also covered the "three last chapters," Alfred also, quite inadvertently and ignorant of his accomplishment, has become the commentator on the *De congelatione et conglutinatione* or *De mineralibus* of Avicenna. This important Arabic treatise was used extensively by almost every Latin scholar who concerned himself with chemical and geological subjects[16] and from it they could derive some clear ideas on the nature of minerals and on the formation of mountains.[17]

In preparing the edition of Alfred's commentary on the *Metheora,* the two manuscripts originally available were Durham, Cathedral Library MS C. III.15, fols. 11v-18r and Paris, Bibliothèque nationale MS Lat. 7131, fols. 82v-85r (limited to book 4). By good fortune this writer discovered an earlier and more accurate text of the commentary as marginalia in Oxford, Bodleian Library MS Selden supra 24, fols. 84r-109r. This Oxford manuscript, containing glosses going beyond book 4 of the *Metheora,* i.e., glosses for Avicenna's *De mineralibus,* thus constitutes a commentary on a different treatise of whose authorship not even Alfred, its commentator, was aware. Nor can there be any doubt that Alfred was indeed the author of this gloss-like commentary on the *De mineralibus*. In his search for "une source inconnue de Roger Bacon,"[18] Auguste Pelzer not only established Alfred as Bacon's source, but his search also took him beyond the fourth book of the *Metheora,* i.e., into the *De mineralibus.* In MS Vatican, Urb. lat. 206, fols. 253r-254r, he found two different sets of glosses attributed to Alfred, e.g.: *secundum alb* or *alf' dicit, al'ved* and even *assub,* all variations of *Alfredus.*[19] These glosses have been thoroughly compared with the anonymous marginal glosses in the Oxford MS (Bodleian, Selden supra 24, fols. 113r-114r), and found to be quite similar, as the specimina in the appendix demonstrate. In other words, Alfred was not misquoted.

But these particular folia of the Oxford manuscript are in an abominable condition. Even an *in situ* examination revealed little beyond what was visible in the microfilm copy. Some pages are smudged, others are illegible because the writing of the reverse side shows through. Even an examination using an ultra-violet lamp met with little success.

Yet in spite of these various problems, MS Selden supra 24 is a very important manuscript and, as far as present knowledge goes, the most complete source for Alfred's commentary on either the *Metheora* or the *De mineralibus.* Since Alfred's glosses are anonymous in this manuscript, and since most of the glosses are in the same hand as the text itself, the thought lies near that Selden supra 24 might be close to the holograph. But the calligraphy showed by text and commentary and the uniform coloration of the ink clearly indicate that it is a copy. It also exhibits the common duality of manuscripts. On the one hand it is messy, with highly abbreviated notes, glosses between lines and in the margins, and letters none-too-neat, but once deciphered, yielding a meaningful text. Such a text is often preferable to the neat, well-executed, legible script of the professional scribe who drops and adds lines, and copies what he sees but does not understand, frequently creating a text devoid of meaning. Fortunately this manuscript is of the former type. Its appearance argues for the scholar, not for the professional scribe. In the *Aristoteles Latinus,*[20] Selden supra 24 is dated "Saec. xii ex. et xiii in.," another reason why it cannot be very far removed from the original in time.

The translation of the *De mineralibus* begins with the incipit: "Terra pura lapis non fit."[21] It consists of three chapters dealing respectively with the formation of stones, mountains, and minerals. Alfred's glosses, however, are limited to expositions about stones on fols. 113r-113v. The *lemmata* are explained in lengthy glosses, many comprising a whole paragraph. Their length is a striking characteristic as compared with the often gloss-like, short notes of the *Metheora* commentary. But even more striking is the absence of any references to Alfred's other works, so frequently found in the *Metheora* commentary, to Aristotle, and to the Latin and Muslim writers cited in the commentary on the *Metheora.* Was this perhaps Alfred's first commentary, written before he could draw, as he did later, upon his many and diverse sources? As with so much else pertaining to Alfred, one cannot be sure at this time.

As stated previously, MS Selden supra 24 is in such poor condition that it has been possible to make only a partial transcription of the glosses. But it is hoped that their transcription, limited though it is, will lead to the discovery of a better preserved text of Alfred's commentary on the *De mineralibus* of Avicenna.

Notes

[1] Clemens Baeumker, *Die Stellung des Alfred von Sareshel (Alfredus Anglicus) und seiner Schrift De motu cordis in der Wissenschaft des beginnenden 13. Jahrhunderts*, Sitzungsberichte der Königlich-Bayerischen Akademie der Wissenschaften 9 (Munich, 1913) Cf. James K. Otte, "The Life and Writings of Alfredus Anglicus," *Viator* 3 (1972), 275-91, and "The Role of Alfred of Sareshel (Alfredus Anglicus) and his Commentary on the *Metheora* in the Reacquisition of Aristotle," *Viator* 7 (1976), 197-209.

[2] S. D. Wingate, *The Mediaeval Latin Versions of the Aristotelian Scientific Corpus with Special Reference to the Biological Works* (London, 1931), p. 56. Cf. *Nicolai damasceni: De plantis*, ed. E. H. F. Meyer, De plantis (Leipzig, 1841).

[3] *Avicennae: De congelatione et conglutinatione lapidum*, being sections of the *Kitâb al-Shifâ'*, ed. E. J. Holmyard and D. C. Mandeville (Paris, 1927), 1-4.

[4] R. James Long, "Alfred of Sareshel's Commentary on the Pseudo-Aristotelian *De plantis*," *Mediaeval Studies* 47 (1985), 125-67.

[5] *Alfred of Sareshel's Commentary on the Metheora of Aristotle*, critical edition with introduction and notes by James K. Otte, Studien und Texte zur Geistesgeschichte des Mittelalters 19 (Leiden, 1988).

[6] H. Omont, "Recherches sur la Bibliothèque de l'eglise cathédrale de Beauvais," *Mémoires de l'Académie des Inscriptions et Belles Lettres* 40 (Paris, 1916), 48 n. 134.

[7] *Des Alfred von Sareshel Schrift De motu cordis*, Beiträge zur Geschichte der Philosophie und Theologie des Mittelalters 23 (Münster, 1923).

[8] In an unmarked codex of Aristotelian manuscripts at the John Walters Library in Baltimore, the following note is found in the margin of a Greek-Latin version of the *De generatione et corruptione*: "Liber Aristotelis translatus ab Henrico Aristippo de greco in latinum, correctus et per capitula distinctus a magistro Alvredo de Saresh(el), secundum commentum Alkindi super eundem librum." George Lacombe, *Alfredus in Metheora*, Beiträge zur Geschichte der Philosophie und Theologie des Mittelalters, supp. 3 (Münster, 1935), p. 464. L. Minio-Palluello, "Henri Aristippe, Guillaume de Moerbeke et les traductions latines medievales des *Météorologiques* et du *De generatione et corruptione* d'Aristote," *Revue Philosophioue de Louvain* 45 (1947), 208-35, demonstrated philosophically that Henry Aristippus could not have been the translator of the Graeco-Latin version of the *De generatione et corruptione*, that the note in the Walters Library is incorrect, and that until its translator can be identified we must classify this translation as anonymous.

[9] Otte, *Alfred of Sareshel's Commentary on the Metheora*, p. 13: "Quare autem vapor et calor invisibiles flammam visibilem producant, in libro *De generatione et corruptione* discussimus."

[10] Lacombe, p. 464.

[11] Alfred of Sareshel, *Commentary on the Metheora of Aristotle* ed. James K. Otte (Leiden, 1988).

[12] See the respective editions by Wingate, Meyer, and Holmyard cited above.

[13] Aristotle, *Meteorologica* 378b5, ed. H. P. D. Lee (London, 1952), p. 289.

[14] To the MSS, Bibliothèque nationale, Lat. 6325; Reims, cod. 682; Nuremberg, MS Cent. V, 59, can be added MS Selden supra 24.

[15] Lacombe, p. 464.

[16] George Sarton, *Introduction to the History of Science* (Baltimore, 1931), 2, pt. 2:511.

[17] Ibid., p. 515.

[18] Auguste Pelzer, "Une source inconnue de Roger Bacon: Alfred de Sareshel, commentateur des Météorologiques d'Aristote," *Archivum Franciscanum Historicum* 12 (1919), 44-67.

[19] Ibid.

[20] *Aristoteles Latinus*, 1:398.

[21] In the five manuscripts that the writer has examined, the incipit of *De mineralibus* or *De congelatione et conglutinatione*: "Terra pura lapis non fit," follows the explicit of book 4 of the *Metheora* without a title or any other sign of division. Cf. MSS Vatican, Urb. Lat. 206, fol. 353r; Oxford, Corpus Christi College C. 114, fol. 110v; and D. 111, fol. 117v; Bodleian, Selden supra 24, fol. 113r; Madrid Escorial, F. II, 4, fol. 309v.

Appendix

The Glosses on Alfred of Sareshel's Commentary on *De congelatione et conglutinatione lapidum*

The following are transcriptions of the incipits and explicits of the eight glosses making up Alfred's commentary on *De mineralibus*. The *lemmata* are printed in italics.

As indicated in the preceding study, Alfred's glosses are cited in MS Urb. Lat. 206. These are by two separate commentators: in the margins by an anonymous scholar, and at the foot of the folia by Adam of Bocfield. A few examples of their references to Alfred (*lemmata* 3 and 4 below) prove his authorship and demonstrate their indebtedness to him.

1. *Terra pura lapis non fit:*
Luto igitur viscoso primum liquiditate per elementares [?] eiecta, sola remanet viscositas cum arrido conglutinata quia mixta sub . . . unde et ultima caliditate ignito arrido liquescit viscositas. (fol. 113r)

2. *eodem modo quo coagulatur sal:*
Sicut enim in primo capitulo sui libri dicit vapor grossus [illegible] aque admixtus facet eam salsam unde et natura eus pars in quolibet loco relicta . . . suntque lenes et vehementer compacta ex vapore frigido sicco. sal vero asperum porosus ex vapore equale. (fol. 113r)

3. *et dicitur lac virginis:*

(a) Commentary by Adam of Bocfield (at the foot of the folia MS Urb. Lat. 206, fol. 253v)

dicit Alfredus quod lac virginis est densum et multum terrestris nature qualiter quod eo ex quibus fiat et etiam cetera coagulata fiant in libro de xij [i.e. XII] aquis dicetur, ut ipse dicit.

(b) Glosses by an anonymous scholar (in the margins of the folio cited)

al<fredus>: lac virginis est valde densum et valde terrestris nature. qualiter et ex quibus fiat et cetera coagulata fiunt, dicetur in libris de xij [i.e. XII] aquis.

(c) Anonymous glosses, i.e., Alfred's glosses in MS Selden supra fol. 24, 113v

[illegible] quibus lac virginis et cum coagulata [illegible] et libro dicet duodecim aquis. . .

4. *quedam vegetabilia et quedam animalia vertuntur in lapides:*

(a) Commentary of Adam of Bocfield (MS Urb. Lat. 206, fol. 254r)

patet per assub [Alfredum] dicentem quod piscis quidam cum extrahitur a mari statim fit lapis. est enim vicossissime substantie caloris expers, nisi tamen tantum quantum ad exilletationem [corr: exilem animatione] sufficit, qui calido equoris conservatur quo per aeris tactum emisso simul cum animatione lapidescit.

(b) Glosses by an anonymous scholar (in the margins, 253v)

al<fredus> quidam piscis cum extrahitur a mari statim fit lapis. quoque est viscose caloris expers nisi tantum quantum ad exilem animationem sufficit qui calido equoris vapore conservatur quo enim tali [?] non emisso simul sum animatione lapidescit.

(c) Anonymous glosses, i.e., Alfred's (MS Selden supra 24, fol. 113v):

Ut piscis quidam cum extrahitur a mare statim fit lapis. . . . Eodem modo convertit [?] ovi alibumen calor.

5. *Estque locus in Arabia:*
Ex solis ad locos [?] vel ad vaporem [illegible] quali [illegible] dispositione ut apparet in eclipsi solis . . . stelle allicuius in ortu corpora [illegible] et funda aque. (fol. 113v)

6. *Panis quoque propre toracem in lapidem conversus est:*
Experit autem corporis liquiditas et dissoluta [illegible] viscositas conservatur coagulata ex frigore. (fol. 113v)

7. *Sepe etiam fiunt lapides ex igne:*
Videtur lactis [?] ex igne cum estinguitur id est amota aut materia viscosa coagulatur. . . . accipet sicut enim corpori ubi [illegible] [illegible] ignis carbonem scilicet luce. (fol. 113v)

8. *Donec residuus fit cinis:*
In harum compactione corporis duplici processu naturam esperat [?] violentia. (fol. 113v)

The Oxford Condemnations of 1277 and the Intellectual Life of the Thirteenth-Century Universities

Leland E. Wilshire

On March 18, 1277, the archbishop of Canterbury, Robert Kilwardby, speaking as "visitor" or patron of Merton College before the assembled students and with the full assent of the University of Oxford faculty, prohibited thirty errors in grammar, logic and natural philosophy.[1] Since this event took place eleven days after a formal address to the University of Paris by Stephen Tempier, bishop of Paris, condemning 219 articles, many modern scholars see 1277 as a great watershed year in the intellectual history of the Middle Ages.

It has been a common assertion by such scholars as Callus, Hinebusch, Crowley, Zavalloni and others that the Oxford Condemnations of 1277 were directed against Thomas Aquinas. From an analysis of the prohibitions themselves, the historical events surrounding the speech, and the later correspondence of Kilwardby with Peter of Conflans, however, it was argued in a predecessor of this present study that Kilwardby's Oxford Condemnations were not written as a direct counter to the specific views of Aquinas at all,[2] but appear rather to deal with the older controversy over plurality/unicity and with issues relevant to the intellectual milieu of Oxford University. This study will review the previous argument, address subsequent criticism, and proceed to look at the broader issue of the relationship of the Oxford Condemnations to the intellectual life of the thirteenth-century universities.

An examination of the Condemnations reveals no specific mention of Aquinas or his followers and there are no specific Thomistic points at issue within them. Furthermore, there is no correspondence between the Oxford Condemnations and the twenty or so propositions Etienne Gilson labels as Thomistic in the Paris Condemnations of the same year.[3] In the first parts of the Oxford prohibitions, the sections on grammar and logic, Kilwardby deals with such issues as whether the noun agrees with the verb, and the correct way to form syllogistic arguments.[4] In the final section on natural philosophy, the archbishop does raise both the hotly debated issue of the *rationes seminales* in man and the problem of whether the human soul is either simple or composite. Although D. A. Callus can find eleven of the sixteen propositions on natural philosophy relating either directly or indirectly to Thomas's thesis of the unicity of substantial form,[5] the propositions can just as easily be seen as part of the general debate raging over these points at the universities of Oxford and Paris over a fifty-year period and peculiar neither to Kilwardby nor to Aquinas.

If one can argue that the issue of unity of form originated with Thomas, then one can say that any criticism of this position must be directed against Aquinas himself. There is a unique Thomistic reformulation of the issue, to be sure, but the broader topic and debate over plurality and unicity of form arising from interpretations of Aristotle and his Islamic and Jewish commentators had been going on for at least a half a century. Thirteenth-century scholars and churchmen had ranged themselves on both sides of this issue. What will have to be considered is whether the unique metaphysical Thomistic "thesis of unicity of substantial form" based upon Thomas's new notion of being is touched upon in Kilwardby's 1277 Condemnations.

The argument shifts to the historical events surrounding the Oxford Condemnations. There is no evidence of any papal correspondence with Archbishop Kilwardby as there is evidence of such correspondence with Bishop Tempier of Paris.[6] It has been asserted that the Oxford speech of Kilwardby set up a serious agitation in the intellectual world with the General Chapter of the Dominicans in 1278 sending delegates to England to investigate those who disparage "the writings of the venerated Friar Thomas Aquinas."[7] The strong reaction in favor of Thomism at Oxford in the writings of Richard Knapwell is additionally cited as an immediate cause of the 1277 Condemnations and, it has been argued, Kilwardby himself was promoted to the cardinalate to "save the old prelate from serious difficulties."[8]

There are difficulties with the relationship of all these later historical events to the 1277 Oxford Condemnations. One can find no disparaging of the writings of Thomas in any of the known works of Kilwardby,[9] and Kilwardby himself had been promoted to the cardinalate a month before the Dominican chapter meeting. The young scholar Knapwell incepted later in 1280 with his provocative works written after this date. Finally, the promotion of Kilwardby to the cardinalate can be seen in the opposite light of strengthening the "conservative" element at the curia with John Peckham, a more strident individual, being made archbishop of Canterbury.

Insight to the relationship of the Oxford Condemnations of 1277 and Thomas Aquinas can be found in the correspondence between Kilwardby and Peter of Conflans, Archbishop of Corinth, a Dominican then residing in Paris and an emerging young disciple of Thomas.[10] No copy of the Conflans epistle to Kilwardby survives, but it appears to have addressed seven points arising directly or indirectly out of the Oxford articles. Buttressing his reply with appeals to Augustine, Aristotle and Averroes, Kilwardby defends his speech as having been a matter of orthodoxy against heresy, true philosophy against that which is manifestly false, and the Christian faith against that which is repugnant to it, but there is no mention of Aquinas. On Conflans raising the issue of the specific Thomistic theory of "unity of substantial form" in his correspondence,

Kilwardby replies in the famous "seventh point" of the letter that "by these words, such an article was not condemned at Oxford nor do I remember hearing of it. Why it is called 'positio de unitate formarum,' I do not sufficiently understand."[11] These are not the words of a person who has directly opposed Thomas in the Oxford Condemnations, but of one who is just learning about this particular interpretive theory in this correspondence with the young disciple of Thomas. Kilwardby now may begin to argue against Aquinas, but that is in this later correspondence and not in the Oxford Condemnations of 1277 themselves. The "seventh point" of Kilwardby's letter seems to have been circulated as an independent thesis.[12] Thus it was concluded in the earlier study that "what is certain is that the Oxford Condemnations of 1277 were not directed, with intent and purpose, against Aquinas."[13]

This thesis was challenged by John F. Wippel of the Catholic University of America in his study of the Paris Condemnations.[14] In his rebuttal, however, Wippel does not deal directly with the Oxford Condemnations themselves, nor with the immediate circumstances surrounding the prohibitions, nor with the correspondence of Kilwardby with Conflans. Rather, he argues from a quotation in a 1310 text of Henry of Harclay that the prohibitions by Kilwardby and the condemnations of Peckham were directed against Thomas's thesis of unicity of substantial form.[15] Henry of Harclay does indeed contain two propositions in paraphrased form from the 1277 Oxford Condemnations although with different numeration. But reference to Kilwardby's prohibitions had been standard practice for polemical Franciscan writers ever since the days of John Peckham.[16] It would have been better to base the argument on the words of Kilwardby himself and on the immediate reaction, than on polemics thirty-five years later.

The argument over the object of Kilwardby's prohibitions raises the broader issue of the relationship of the Oxford Condemnations of 1277 to the intellectual climate of the thirteenth century universities, especially that of the University of Oxford. In October of 1284, John Peckham, by then archbishop of Canterbury, upon the death of Kilwardby, summoned the masters of Oxford to the abbey of Osney, where he verbally renewed Kilwardby's Oxford Condemnations along with an additional condemnation against the unity of form.[17] Peckham had earlier, in 1270, personally challenged Aquinas to a disputation on unity of form when both were at the University of Paris. Thomas seems to have gotten the better of that exchange and, for various reasons, unity of form was never condemned at Paris.[18]

The Dominicans at Oxford resented Peckham's action at Osney as specifically directed against them, with their prior making a formal protest. In response to this action, Peckham, in a letter dated November 10, 1284, asked the chancellor of Oxford to investigate the full list of propositions prohibited by Kilwardby, the penalties prescribed, the names of those who had been compelled to recant, and of those who defended them or dared still to defend any of them.[19] The propositions were to be re-examined by a panel of theologians. Peckham's comments on penalties and the names of those compelled to recant show no direct familiarity with Kilwardby's 1277 prohibitions, as this is not the form in which they were issued. It is interesting that Peckham not only felt obliged to add an additional statement on unity of form in this renewal of Kilwardby's articles, but that he also listed theological arguments against unity of form not found in earlier condemnations: (1) that Christ's body was not one and the same before and after death and (2) that the relics of the saints venerated in Rome and all Christendom did not in reality appertain to their own natural bodies.

What can be learned from the later documents is that Peckham did not have Kilwardby's prohibitions in his possession nor did he know exactly what was in them. He tried to make up for this omission with letters, dated November 14, 1284, to the chancellor of the University of Oxford and Master Fleckham of the school of theology, asking them if they would "carefully but quietly and without raising the alarm" find what errors Kilwardby had condemned and the penalties prescribed by him for continuing to uphold them, whether any proceedings had been taken against anyone for defending them, and whether anyone was still maintaining them in defiance of his own decree.[20]

A full report was to be back to Peckham by St. Nicholas's feast. Alas, no report was forthcoming. On December 7, 1284, the archbishop sent additional letters to the chancellor and to Master Fleckham censuring them for their neglect of his letters.[21] In a letter about his meeting with the Dominican prior, Peckham speaks of the "childish disputations" at Oxford which his predecessor had censured.[22]

This situation continued for three years into the year 1287. Peckham still had not laid his hands on what he believed to be Kilwardby's Oxford Condemnations of 1277. Early in 1287 Peckham received a papal mandate requesting him to send to the curia a copy of Kilwardby's 1277 prohibitions. Peckham obviously did not have these, for in March of that year he sent an urgent letter to the bishop of Lincoln demanding information in regard to Kilwardby's prohibitions and any penal measure which had resulted from them.[23] In this letter Peckham acknowledges to the bishop of Lincoln that he had acted negligently in omitting to see the much needed information during his visitation at Oxford. This situation would be humorous were it not for the tragic effects it had upon scholars and scholarly inquiry. Peckham's negligence, for instance, had not hindered him, in the previous year, from including references to Kilwardby's prohibitions in his excommunication of Richard Knapwell (Clapwell) as found in the *Annals of Dunstable*.[24]

It may be well here to explore the exact prohibitive nature of Kilwardby's 1277 Oxford Condemnations. Are they really condemnations? The Paris Condemnations of 1270 and 1277 were statements of canonical condemnation by the bishop of Paris, with excommunication threatened for those who persisted in its errors. Peckham's later usage of Kilwardby's Oxford Condemnations of 1277, with his own addition, and his excommunication of Richard Knapwell, in 1286, were also official ecclesiastical actions.

In his letter to Peter of Conflans, Kilwardby makes the point that his 1277 Oxford Condemnations were of a different nature. He repudiates categorically that he had condemned any thesis. His was not a condemnation in the canonical sense of the word in the manner in which heresies were usually censured, but a mere prohibition to teach, or to maintain certain tenets with "pertinacity" in the schools, that is, at the university.[25]

This perceived opening for academic discussion, so long as it is not done with "pertinacity," was picked up later by Richard Knapwell in his running controversy with Archbishop Peckham. In his *Quaestiones ordinariae,* Knapwell distinguishes between a condemnation and a prohibition and strongly denies that the thesis of unity of form, argued by him, had ever been condemned as heretical.[26] He makes the additional point that all the masters of the University of Oxford, regents and non-regents, who were in town at the time and took part at the General Congregation assembled for this purpose, bear witness that this opinion was not condemned. Knapwell argues that he was just exercising his undoubted right as a master to discuss the issue in a cautious fashion as allowed by the restriction, and ends his work with the words,

> All this is said without pertinacity and without injury or detriment to a better opinion, lest we ascribe to the human nature united to the Word something not belonging to it, or do not attribute something which belongs to it, and thus be found false witnesses of the Word incarnate of the Virgin.[27]

This appeal to free academic discussion, with its "pertinacity" caveat, did not save Knapwell. On April 30, 1286, Archbishop Peckham with his suffragens, selected eight theses taken from the writings of Knapwell, including a statement of the thesis of unity of form, and excommunicated all those who maintained them.[28] Included among the accusations was the alarming statement that Knapwell had rejected the Church Fathers and had appealed only to the Bible and direct experience. Knapwell gave repeated public details of this radical accusation.

Knapwell set out for the papal court to defend himself in person. As he passed through Paris, his case aroused considerable interest and sympathy in the academic community. In one of his quodlibets the Parisian scholar, Godfrey of Fontaines, described Knapwell as a "certain valiant master."[29] Godfrey was probably voicing a general feeling among the Parisian academic community when he declared that it was extraordinary that any single individual should take upon himself to censure a theory which many contemporary theologians, at least at Paris, had asserted to be neither erroneous nor heretical. When Knapwell arrived in Rome, however, he found that a new pope, Nicholas IV, a former Franciscan minister general and an old friend of Peckham, was on the papal throne. Knapwell was ordered never again to discuss the subject of unity of form and departed to a house of his order in Bologna.

History is never tidy. There were further endings to these events of the intellectual life of the early universities. Contrary to Peckham's expectation, Rome ultimately did not ratify his condemnation of unity of form. There is evidence that Knapwell disobeyed his restriction of silence. The radical theologian Thomas Aquinas was canonized by John XXII in 1323 and Stephen de Bounet, a later bishop of Paris, in 1327, annulled those portions of the Paris Condemnations of 1277 that he felt attacked the views of Aquinas.[30]

More importantly, the issue of the restriction on academic inquiry at the universities was being stretched and challenged. Although the excommunication process was cumbersome and not entirely predictable, there were some celebrated victims such as Knapwell. That it did have a chilling effect on some scholarship can be seen in the complaints of the Oxford master John Baconthorpe, who commented that to him there appeared to be more freedom at the University of Paris than there was at Oxford, and spoke of his submission to the condemnations of Peckham.[31] There were scholars at Paris, like Giles of Rome, who might have reversed the analysis. Giles went into temporary exile from the academic center of Paris rather than repudiate his errors arising from the Paris Condemnations of 1277.[32] Even with these complaints, however, the universities became arenas of intellectual inquiry. There is the strange situation that because of the local nature of the condemnations, it was allowable to discuss the issue of unity of form at the University of Paris as it was to discuss the issue of the eternity of the world at Oxford. One could travel to where there was freedom to promote one's view. The cumbersome nature of the use of excommunication was also not lost on scholars. Knapwell's associates, Robert of Orford, Thomas of Sutton and William of Macclesfield, continued the controversy over unity of form at Oxford, seemingly challenging further usage of the excommunication process. By 1303, Nicholas Trivet treated the restrictions with humor. To an objector who argued that many difficulties would follow from the Pluralist theory, Trivet answered that since the archbishop (Peckham) did not tell us how to solve the difficulties against his view, neither would he tell the objector lest he misrepresent the archbishop.[33] The "watershed" of these years of the early universities was not so much in their condemnations and restrictions, but in the emerging intellectual setting of the openness of inquiry. It is out of this emerging academic freedom at the early universities that Fernand van Steenberghen can call this last quarter of the thirteenth century perhaps "the richest and most productive period of scholasticism."[34]

Notes

[1] *Chartularium Universitatis Parisiensis*, ed. H. Denifle and A. Chatelain (Paris, 1889), 1:558-60. I have included an English translation of Kilwardby's Oxford Condemnations of 1277 as an appendix to this present study.

[2] Leland E. Wilshire, "Were the Oxford Condemnations Directed Against Aquinas?" *New Scholasticism, Aquinas Septicentennial Edition 48* (1974), 125-32. Scholarship has benefited from the recent edited editions of various works by Kilwardby: Daniel A. Callus O.P., "The 'Tabulae

super originalia patrum' of Robert Kilwardby O.P.," *Studia Mediaevalia in Honorem R. J. Martin* (Bruges, 1948); *De ortu scientiarum*, ed. Albert G. Judy (Oxford, 1976); H.-F. Dondaine O.P., "Le 'De 43 quaestionibus' de Robert Kilwardby," *Archivum Fratrum Praedicatorum* 47 (1977), 5-50; *De natura relationis*, ed. Lorenz Schmücker (Brixen, 1980); *Quaestiones in librum tertium sententiarum I. Christologie*, ed. Elizabeth Gössmann (Munich, 1982); *Quaestiones in librum tertium sententiarum II. Tugendlehre*, ed. Gerhard Leibold (Munich, 1985); *Quaestiones in librum primum*, ed. Johannes Schneider (Munich, 1986); *On Time and Imagination, De tempore, De spiritu Fantastico*, ed. P. Osmund Lewry O.P. (Oxford, 1987).

[3] Etienne Gilson, *The History of Christian Philosophy in the Middle Ages* (New York, 1955), p. 728.

[4] Cf P. Osmund Lewry O.P., "The Oxford Condemnations of 1277 in Grammar and Logic," *English Logic and Semantics from the End of the Twelfth Century to the Time of Ockham and Burleigh*, ed. H. A. G. Braakhuis, C. H. Kneepkens and L. M. de Rijk (Nijmegen, 1981), pp. 235-78. As it seemed impossible to trace the grammatical and logical positions to their original proponents, Lewry attempted the limited task of comparing the Oxford grammatical and logical works from the second half of the thirteenth century with the prohibitions of Kilwardby. At the end of the study, he speaks of the modest results of the survey, although there are some intriguing hints of the influence of teachings of Boethius of Dacia upon certain scholars at Oxford. In the logical propositions, Lewry suggests that a work by John de Secceheville (1265), an Oxford master influenced heavily by Averroes, may also lie behind some of the prohibitions of Kilwardby.

[5] Daniel A. Callus, *The Condemnations of St. Thomas at Oxford* (Oxford, 1955).

[6] For a follow-up papal letter to Tempier, see *Chartularium*, 1:541-42; A. Callebaut, "Jean Peckham et l'augustinisme. Aperçus historiques," *Archivum Franciscanum Historicum* 18 (1925), 459-60.

[7] Maur Burbach, "Early Dominican and Franciscan Legislation Regarding St. Thomas," *Mediaeval Studies* 4 (1942), 141.

[8] Ellen M. F. Sommer-Seckendorff, *Studies in the Life of Robert Kilwardby* (Rome, 1937), p. 129.

[9] Henry F. Nardone, in his unpublished doctoral dissertation, states that "Bishop Kilwardby went as far as to grant forty days indulgence to anyone who would abstain from propounding this "nefarious doctrine of Brother Thomas." Henry F. Nardone, "St. Thomas Aquinas and the Condemnations of 1277" (unpublished doctoral dissertation, The Catholic University of America, Washington, D.C., 1963), p. 75. Nardone gives no citation for this assertion.

[10] MSS containing the first six points were collated and published by Franz Ehrle, "Ein Schreiben des Erzbishofs von Canterbury, Robert Kilwardby zur Rechtfertigung seiner Lehverurtheilung vom 18. März 1277," *Beiträge zur Geschichte der mittelalterlichen Scholastik II. Der Augustinismus und der Aristotelismus in der Scholastik gegen Ende des 13. Jahrhunderts, Archiv für Literatur und Kirchengeschichte des Mittelalters* 5 (1889), 614. Recently discovered MSS containing the seventh point were collated and published by Birkenmajer, "Der Brief Robert Kilwardbys an Peter von Conflans und die Streitschrift des Ägidius von Lessines," *Vermischte Untersuchungen zur Geschichte der Mittelalterlichen Philosophie*, *Beiträge* 20, no. 5 (1922), 46-69.

[11] Birkenmajer, *Beiträge* 20, No. 5 (1922), 60: "Sub his quidem verbis articulus iste non erat Oxonie prohibitus, nec illum memini me audivisse. Quare autem dicitur 'positio de unitate formarum,' non satis intelligo."

[12] The Stams Catalogue of 1325 credits Kilwardby with a work entitled *De unitate formarum*. It may possibly be the name attached to this "seventh point" as it circulated among scholars. G. Meersseman, O.P., *Laurentii Pignon Catalogi et Chronica, Accedunt Catalogi Stamensis et Upsalensis Scriptorum O.P.*, Monumenta Ordinis Fratrum Praedicatorum Historica 18 (Rome, 1936), 57. Cf. Daniel A. Callus O.P., "The 'Tabulae super originalia patrum' of Robert Kilwardby O.P.," *Studia Mediaevalia in Honorem R. J. Martin* (Bruges, 1948), 244-45.

[13] Wilshire, "Were the Oxford Condemnations Directed Against Aquinas?" p. 132.

[14] John F. Wippel, "The Condemnations of 1270 and 1277 at Paris," *Journal of Medieval and Renaissance Studies* 7 (1977), 169-201.

[15] Armand Maurer C.S.B., "Henry of Harclay's Disputed Question on the Plurality of Forms," *Essays in Honour of Anton Charles Pegis*, ed. J. Reginald O'Donnell C.S.B. (Toronto, 1974), 125-60.

[16] See also references to Kilwardby's 1277 Condemnations in the fourteenth-century writer Walter Catton. Jeremiah O'Callaghan S.J., "The Second Question of the Prologue to Walter Catton's Commentary on the Sentences on Intuitive and Abstractive Knowledge," *Nine Medieval Thinkers, A Collection of Hitherto Unedited Texts*, ed. J. Reginald O'Donnell C.S.B. (Toronto, 1955), 233-61.

[17] *Annales de Oseneia, Annales Monastici* 4, ed. H.R. Luard, (Rolls Series) (London, 1869), 297-99. Although Peckham continually complains that he does not have a copy of Kilwardby's 1277 Condemnations, the Osney annalist includes a paraphrased copy of the articles.

[18] V. Sist, "The Second Regency of St. Thomas at Paris," *Reality* (Dubuque, Iowa, 1961), 1-11.

[19] *Memorandum, Reg. J. de Pontissara, Episcopi Wyntoniensis*, ed. C. Deedes (London, 1915), 1:307-8; *Registrum Epistolarum J. Pecham, Archiepiscopi Cantuariensis*, ed. C. T. Martin (Rolls Series) (London, 1885), 3:840-43.

[20] Peckham, *Epistolae*, 3:852-53: "Sine scandalo et tumultu inquiratis sollicite qui sunt articuli universi quos damnasse dicitur tantus pater."

[21] Ibid., 3:862-63.

[22] Ibid., 3:866: "Aliud igitur est quod de scriptis theologicis est Romanae celsitudini reservatum Parisius, ab eo quod inventum Oxoniae in certaminibus puerilibus per praedecessoris nostri sapientiam est damnatum."

[23] Ibid., 3:944-45.

[24] *Annales Prioratus de Dunstaphia, Annales Monastici*, ed. H. R. Luard (Rolls Series) (London, 1866), 3:325.

[25] Ehrle, *Beiträge*, p. 614: "Alias dogmatizando talia asserendi."

[26] Richard Knapwell, *Quaestiones ordinariae*, Bologna, Biblioteca Universitaria, MS 1539 (fol. 51ra-54vb). Cf F. Pelster, "Richard von Knapwell O.P., seine *Quaestiones disputatae* und sein *Quodlibet*," *Zeitschrift für katholische Theologie*, 52 (1928), 491.

[27] Knapwell, *Quaestiones ordinariae*, 54vb.

[28] Peckham, *Epistolae*, 3:921-23.

[29] *Les quatre premiers quodlibets de Godefroid des Fontaines*, ed. M. de Wulf and A. Pelzer (Louvain, 1904), p. 198.

[30] *Chartularium*, 2:281 n. 838.

[31] *Johannis Bachonis Quaestiones in Tertium et Quartum Libros Sententiarum* (Cremona, 1618), pp. 119-24: "Haec dicta sunt sequendo adiculos supra positos. Si autem aliquod dictis, vel de dicendis, repugnaret illis, vel alicui de articulis domini Joh. de Pecham pro non dicto habeatur"; quoted in Daniel A. Callus, "The Problem of the Unity of Form and Richard Knapwell O.P.," *Mélanges offerts a Étienne Gilson* (Toronto and Paris, 1959), p. 159.

[32] *Chartularium*, 1:633. Cf. Francis E. Kelley, "Robert Orford's Attack on Giles of Rome," *The Thomist* 51 (1987), 70-96.

[33] F. Ehrle, "Nikolaus Trivet," *Festgabe Clemens Baeumker*, (Münster, 1923), p. 23 n. 1. Cf. D. A. Callus, "Richard Knapwell," p. 159.

[34] Fernand van Steenberghen, *The Philosophical Movement in the Thirteenth Century* (Edinburgh, 1955), p. 105.

Appendix

The Oxford Condemnations of 1277 of Robert Kilwardby: An English Translation

Chartularium Universitatis Parisiensis, H. Denifle and E. Chatelain, eds., 1, (Paris, 1889-1897), 558-60.

In grammaticalibus
Errors in Grammar

1. *Ego currit, tu currit, currit et curro eque sunt perfecte et congrue orationes. Similiter currens est ego.*
   [It is false in grammar to say] "I" (1st person) "runs" (3rd person) or "you" (2nd person) "runs" (3rd person). One cannot equally use "he is running" and "I am running" to mean the same thing in proper and normal speech. Likewise one cannot use the ungrammatical statement "I" (1st person) "is running" (3rd person).

2. *Item Socratis legere, Socrati legere sicut Socratem legere.*
   Again [it is false to say] "to read of Socrates," (gen.), "to read to Socrates" (dat.), and have it mean the same as "to read Socrates" (acc.).

3. *Item quod verbum manens verbum potest privari omnibus accidentibus.*
   Again [it is false to say] a verb deprived of all of its accidents can still remain a verb.

4. *Item quod nullum nomen est tertie persone.*
   Again [it is false to say] that any noun is of the "third person."

In logicalibus
Errors in Logic

1. *Quod contraria simul possunt esse vera in aliqua materia.*
   [It is false in logic] that contraries can be simultaneously true in some material.

2. *Item quod sillogismus peccans in materia non est sillogismus.*
   Again [it is false] that the syllogism which is materially defective is not a syllogism.

3. *Item quod non est suppositio in propositione magis pro supposito quam pro significato, et ideo idem est dicere, cujuslibet hominis asinus currit, et asinus cujuslibet hominis currit.*
   Again [it is false] that a supposition in a major premise can come before a supposition that gives it connotation, in this instance, when "any given ass of a man runs" would mean the same as "the ass of any given man runs."

4. *Item quod animal est omnis homo.*
   Again [it is false to state in logic], "animal is all men."

5. *Item quod signum non distribuit subjectum in comparatione ad predicatum.*
   Again [it is false] that a sign does not distribute the subject in relation to the predicate.

6. *Item quod veritas cum necessitate tantum est cum constancia subjecti.*
   Again [it is false] that necessary truth depends on persistence of the subject.

7. *Item quod non est ponere demonstracionem sine rebus entibus.*
   Again [it is false] that nothing is proved by demonstration without evidence of existence.

8. *Item quod omnis propositio de futuro vera est necessaria.*
   Again [it is false] that every proposition about the future is necessary.

9. *Item quod terminus cum verbo de presenti distribuitur pro omnibus differentiis temporum.*
   Again [it is false] that a term with a verb in the present is distributed for all differences of time.

10. *Item quod ex negativa de predicato finito sequitur affirmativa de predicato infinito sine constancia subjecti.*
    Again [it is false] that the affirmative about the infinite predicate follows from the negative of finite predicate without agreement with the subject.

In naturalibus
Errors in Natural Philosophy

1. *Item quod quot sunt composita, tot principia omnino prima.*
   Again [it is false in natural philosophy] that there are as many completely first principles as there are composites.

2. *Item quod forma corrumpitur in pure nichil.*
Again [it is false] that form is destroyed into pure nothingness.

3. *Item quod nulla potentia activa est in materia.*
Again [it is false] that there is no active potency in matter.

4. *Item quod privatio est pure nichil, et quod est in corporibus supra celestibus et hiis inferioribus.*
Again [it is false] that privation is pure nothingness and that it is both in bodies above the heavens and below it.

5. *Item quod est conversiva generatio animalium sicut elementorum.*
Again [it is false] that the elements regenerate the same as the animals.

6. *Item quod vegetativa, sensitiva et intellectiva sunt simul in embrione tempore.*
Again [it is false] that the vegetative, the sensitive and the intellective [forms] co-exist simultaneously in the embryo.

7. *Item quod intellectiva introducta corrumpitur sensitiva et vegetativa.*
Again [it is false] that when the intellective [form] comes to be, the sensitive and the vegetative [forms] pass away.

8. *Item quod substantia prima non est composita nec simplex.*
Again [it is false] that primal substance is neither composite nor simple.

9. *Item quod tempus non est in predicamento quantitatis.*
Again [it is false] that time is not in a category of quantity.

10. *Item quod non est inventum ab Aristotele, quod intellectiva manet post separacionem.*
Again [it is false] that Aristotle did not originate the statement that the intellectual principle remains after the point of death.

11. *Item quod quando incompletum fit completum, diversificant essentiam; set quando incompletum fit sub completo, tunc non.*
Again [it is false] that when the incomplete becomes complete, there is an essential diversification, but when the incomplete never reaches a complete state, there is not a diversification.

12. *Item quod vegetativa, sensitiva et intellectiva sint una forma simplex.*
Again [it is false] that the vegetative, the sensitive and the intellective principles are one simple form.

13. *Item quod corpus vivum et mortuum est equivoce corpus, et corpus mortuum secundum quod corpus mortuum sit corpus secundum quid.*
Again [it is false] that body is predicated only equivocally of a living and a dead body, and a dead body, as such, is a body only from a certain point of view.

14. *Item quod materia et forma non distinguantur per essentiam.*
Again [it is false] that matter and form are not essentially distinguished from each other.

15. *Item quod causa prima est ordinabilis in genere, tamen est extra genus.*
Again [it is false] that the primal cause is ordinarily in kind, nevertheless is still beyond kind.

16. *Item quod intellectiva unitur materie prime ita quod corrumpitur illud quod precessit usque ad materiam primam.*
Again [it is false] that the intellective principle is united to prime matter in such a way that all preceding forms are destroyed.

CONTRIBUTORS

SIR RICHARD W. SOUTHERN, formerly of St. John's College in Oxford, is editor of the Oxford series *Auctores Britannici Medii Aevi* and a foremost authority on Grosseteste. Among his many works are *The Making of the Middle Ages* (1953) and *Medieval Humanism* (1970). His latest book, *Robert Grosseteste: The Growth of an English Mind in the Middle Ages*, has been hailed as a milestone of excellence in medieval scholarship.

SERVUS GIEBEN, O.F.M. Cap., of the Istituto Storico dei Cappuccini in Rome, is an authority on Thomas Gascoigne and Robert Grosseteste. He collaborated with Professor Dales on the critical edition of Grosseteste's *Hexaëmeron*, and among the latest of his many works on the bishop is "The Influence of Grosseteste on the Evolution of the Franciscan Order" (1987).

JAMES MCEVOY is *Professeur ordinaire* of Medieval Philosophy at the Institut Supèrieur de Philosophie of the Université Catholique de Louvain, Belgium, and Scientific Director of that university's Centre de Wulf-Mansion. In 1982 he was elected a Member of the Irish National Academy, and he has been a *Stipendiat* of the Alexander von Humboldt-Stiftung (Bonn) at the University of Munich in 1980-1981, and again in 1985. Author of about sixty articles on ancient and medieval thought, and of a book on *The Philosophy of Robert Grosseteste* (Oxford, 1982), he is currently preparing a critical edition of Grosseteste's *Commentary on the Epistle to the Galatians* for the British Academy.

ELWOOD E. MATHER, III, the most recent here of Professor Dales's doctoral graduates, produced a critical edition of *Lecturae in Epistolam ad Romanos V-XVI*, a work ascribed to Robert Grosseteste, as his dissertation. His research of late includes ecclesiastical reform movements in both the thirteenth and sixteenth centuries. He is Assistant Professor of History at Eastern Montana College.

GLENN M. EDWARDS is Adjunct Professor of History at the Borough of Manhattan Community College in New York. He has been a recipient of two graduate awards and of a visiting fellowship to Yale University. Pursuing his interest in the works of Michael Scot, his "The Two Redactions of Michael Scot's *Liber introductorius*" was published in *Traditio* in 1985.

GUNAR FREIBERGS teaches as Professor of History at Los Angeles Valley College in Van Nuys, California. Two of his articles, "The Knowledge of Greek in Western Europe in the Fourteenth Century," and "*Ad orientem hiemalem*: The Saga of a Circuitous Quest for 'A Very Unusual Post-Classical Construction,'" appeared in *Studies in Medieval and Renaissance History* and *Terrae Incognitae*, respectively, in 1989.

R. JAMES LONG is Professor of Philosophy at Fairfield University and secretary-treasurer of the Society for Medieval and Renaissance Philosophy. The recipient of numerous academic honors, he has published three books and more than twenty articles. His most recent publication is a book he edited entitled *Philosophy and the God of Abraham. Essays in Memory of James A. Weisheipl, O.P.* (Toronto, 1991). Currently he is engaged in editing Richard Fishacre's Sentences-Commentary for the Bavarian Academy of Sciences.

JAMES K. OTTE is a Professor of History at the University of San Diego. He has authored several articles on medieval science, and his latest work, an edition of *Alfred of Sareshel's Commentary on the Metheora of Aristotle*, was published by E.J. Brill in 1988.

LELAND E. WILSHIRE is Professor of History at Biola University in La Mirada, California, and has the distinction of being Professor Dales's first graduate student. He is the recipient of several academic honors, has published a number of articles on medieval intellectual history, and his most recent work, "Siger of Brabant in Paradise: Radicalism and Structure in the Medieval University," appeared in *The Intellectual Climate of the Medieval University* in 1990.

A BIBLIOGRAPHY OF THE WORKS OF RICHARD C. DALES

Books:

1. *Roberti Grosseteste Commentarius in VIII Libros Physicorum Aristotelis*. Boulder: University of Colorado Press, 1963

2. *The Achievement of Medieval Science*. Philadelphia: University of Pennsylvania Press, 1973

3. *Marius on the Elements, An Edition with English Translation*. Berkeley and Los Angeles: University of California Press, 1976

4. *The Intellectual Life of Western Europe in the Middle Ages*. Washington, D.C.: University Press of America, 1980; 2nd revised ed., Leiden: E. J. Brill, 1992

5. *Robert Grosseteste, Hexaëmeron*. Auctores Britannici Medii Aevi 6. London: Oxford University Press, 1982 (with Servus Gieben)

6. *Robert Grosseteste, De cessatione legalium*. Auctores Britannici Medii Aevi 7. London: Oxford University Press, 1986 (with Edward B. King)

7. *Robert Grosseteste, De decem mandatis*. Auctores Britannici Medii Aevi 10. London: Oxford University Press, 1987 (with Edward B. King)

8. *Robert Grosseteste's Glosses on the Pauline Epistles*. London: Oxford University Press, (with James McEvoy) (in press)

9. *Medieval Discussions of the Eternity of the World*. Leiden: E.J. Brill, 1990

10. *Medieval Latin Texts on the Eternity of the World*. Leiden, E.J. Brill, 1991

Articles:

1. "Robert Grosseteste's *Commentarius in VIII Libros Physicorum Aristotelis*," *Medievalia et Humanistica* 11 (1957), 10-33

2. "Robert Grosseteste's Scientific Works," *Isis* 52 (1961), 381-407

3. "The *Quaestio de fluxu et refluxu maris* Attributed to Robert Grosseteste," *Speculum* 37 (1962), 582-88

4. "Robert Grosseteste's Treatise *De finitate motus et temporis*," *Traditio* 19 (1963), 245-66

5. "A Note on Grosseteste's *Hexameron*," *Medievalia et Humanistica* 15 (1963), 69-73

6. "The Authorship of the *Summa in Physica* Attributed to Robert Grosseteste," *Isis* 55 (1964), 70-74

7. "Anonymi *De elementis*: From a Twelfth-Century Collection of Scientific Works in British Museum MS Cotton Galba E. IV," *Isis* 56 (1965), 174-89

8. "Grosseteste, Aristotle, and Astronomy, A Manuscript in the Hoose Library," *Coranto* 2 (1965), 7-12

9. "R. de Staningtona: An Unknown Writer of the Thirteenth Century," *Journal of the History of Philosophy* 4 (1966), 199-208

10. "An Unnoticed Translation of Nemesius' *De natura hominis*," *Medievalia et Humanistica* 17 (1966), 13-19

11. "The Text of Grosseteste's Treatise on the Tides, With English Translation," *Isis* 57 (1966), 455-74

12. "Grosseteste's Views on Astrology," *Mediaeval Studies* 29 (1967), 357-63

13. "The Prooemium to Robert Grosseteste's *Hexaemeron*," *Speculum* 43 (1968), 451-61 (with Servus Gieben)

14. "The Influence of Grosseteste's *Hexaemeron* on the *Sentences* Commentaries of Richard Rufus, O.F.M. and Richard Fishacre, O.P.," *Viator* 2 (1971), 271-300

15. "Marius 'On the Elements'" and the Twelfth-Century Science of Matter," *Viator* 3 (1972), 191-218

16. "Adam Marsh, Grosseteste, and the Treatise on the Tides," *Speculum* 52 (1977), 900-902

17. "A Medieval View of Human Dignity," *Journal of the History of Ideas* 38 (1977), 557-72

18. "A Twelfth-Century Concept of the Natural Order," *Viator* 9 (1978), 179-92

19. "The De-Animation of the Heavens in the Middle Ages," *Journal of the History of Ideas* 41 (1980), 531-50

20. "The Use of Thierry of Chartres' *Hexaemeron* by Anonymi *De elementis* and Robert Grosseteste," *Journal of the Rocky Mountain Medieval and Renaissance Association* 1 (1980), 11-20

21. "Discussions of the Eternity of the World During the First Half of the Twelfth Century," *Speculum* 57 (1982), 495-508

22. "Maimonides and Boethius of Dacia on the Eternity of the World," *The New Scholasticism* 56 (1982), 306-19

23. "Henry of Harclay on Infinite Sets," *Journal of the History of Ideas* 45 (1984), 295-301

24. "The Origins of the Doctrine of the Double Truth," *Viator* 15 (1984), 169-79

25. "The Text of Henry of Harclay's *Quaestio Utrum Mundus Potuit Fieri ab Eterno*," *Archives d' histoire doctrinale et littéraire du moyen âge* 51 (1983), 267-99

26. "Friar Arlotto of Prato on the Eternity of the World," *Collectanea Franciscana* 56 (1986), 37-51

27. "The MSS of Robert Grosseteste's *De cessatione legalium*," *Manuscripta* 28 (1984), 3-15 (with Edward B. King)

28. "Fratris Eustachii Atrebatensis *Quaestiones septem de aeternitate*, 1-3," *Archives d' histoire doctrinale et littéraire du moyen âge* 55 (1986), 111-37 (with Omar Argerami)

29. "Robert Grosseteste's Place in Medieval Discussions of the Eternity of the World," *Speculum* 61 (1986), 544-63

30. "Early Thirteenth-Century Discussions of the Eternity of the World," *Traditio* 43 (1987), 171-97

31. Fratris Eustachii Atrebatensis *Quaestiones septem de aeternitate,* 4-7," *Archives d' histoire doctrinale et littéraire du moyen âge* 56 (1987), 59-102 (with Omar Argerami)

32. "Time and Eternity in the Thirteenth Century," *Journal of the History of Ideas* 49 (1988), 27-45

33. "The Computistical Works Ascribed to Robert Grosseteste," *Isis* 8 (1989), 74-79

34. "Robert Grosseteste's Doctrine of the Soul's Care for the Body," *The Warburg Institute Colloquium on Robert Grosseteste* (in press)

35. "Philip the Chancellor on the Eternity of the World," *Essays in Medieval History Presented to Edward B. King*, ed. Robert Benson and Eric W. Naylor (Sewanee, Tenn: Press of the University of the South, 1989)

36. "The Friars and the Eternity of the World," *Monks, Nuns, and Friars in Medieval Society*, ed. Edward B. King, Jacqueline Schaefer and William B. Wadley (Sewanee, Tenn: Press of the University of the South, 1989), 63-70

37. "Some Effects of the Judaeo-Christian Concept of Deity on Medieval Treatments of Classical Problems," *Sewanee Medieval Studies* (accepted)

38. "Gilbert of Stratton. An Early Oxford Defense of Aquinas's Teaching on the Possibility of a Beginningless World," (in progress)

INDEX

AMS Studies in the Middle Ages, No. 23
ISSN: 0270-6261

Other titles in this series:

1. Josiah C. Russell. *Twelfth Century Studies,* 1978.
2. Joachin Bumke. *The Concept of Knighthood in the Middle Ages*. Trans. W.T.H. Jackson and Erika Jackson. 1982.
3. Donald K. Fry. *Norse Sagas Translated into English: A Bibliography*. 1980.
4. Clifford Davidson, C.J. Gianakaris, and John Stroupe, eds. *Drama in the Middle Ages,* 1982.
5. Clifford Davidson. *From Creation to Doom: The York Cycle of Mystery Plays*. 1984.
6. Edith Yenal. *Charles d'Orléans: A Bibliography of Primary and Secondary Sources*. 1984.
7. Joel T. Rosenthal. *Anglo-Saxon History: An Annotated Bibliography, 450-1066*. 1985.
8. Theodore John Rivers. *Laws of Salian and Ripuarian Franks*. 1988.
9. R.C. Famiglietti. *Royaı Intrigue: Crisis at the Court of Charles VI, 1392-1420*. 1986.
10. Barry Gaines. Sir Thomas Malory: *An Anecdotal Bibliography of Editions, 1485-1985*. 1990.
11. Milla Cozart Riggio, ed. *The Wisdom Symposium*. 1986.
12. Josiah Cox Russell. *Medieval Demography*. 1988.
13. J. Bard McNulty. *The Narrative Art of the Bayeux Tapestry Master*. 1989.
15. Donald Gilman, ed. *Everyman and Company: Essays on the Theme and Structure of the European Moral Play*. 1989.
16. Clifford Davidson. *Visualizing the Moral Life: Medieval Iconography and the Macro Moralities*. 1989.
17. Deborah M. Sinnreich-Levi and Gale Sigal, eds. *Voices in Translation: The Authority of "Olde Bookes" in Medieval Literature: Essays in Honor of Helaine Newstead*. 1991.
18. Clifford Davidson and John H. Stroupe, eds. *Drama in the Middle Ages: Second Series*. 1991.

DATE DUE